ANIMA

An Anatomy of a Personified Notion

ANIMA

An Anatomy of a Personified Notion

James Hillman

with excerpts from the writings of
C. G. Jung
and original drawings by Mary Vernon

Spring Publications, Inc.
Dallas, Texas

Published by Spring Publications, Inc.; Box 222069; Dallas, Texas 75222
Printed in the United States of America

International Distributors:
Spring; Postfach; 8800 Thalwil; Switzerland.
Japan Spring Sha, Inc.; 1-2-4, Nishisakaidani-Cho;
Ohharano, Nishikyo-Ku; Kyoto, 610-11, Japan.
Element Books Ltd; Longmead; Shaftesbury;
Dorset SP7 8PL; England.

Library of Congress Cataloging-in-Publication Data

Hillman, James.
    Anima : an anatomy of a personified notion.

    Bibliography: p.
    1. Anima (Psychoanalysis)   2. Jung, C. G. (Carl
Gustav), 1875-1961. I. Jung, C. G. (Carl Gustav),
1875-1961. II. Title.
BF175.5.A52H55   1985   150.19'54   85-18320
ISBN 0-88214-316-6

Third Printing 1987

ACKNOWLEDGMENTS

Cover design by Catherine Meehan and Sven Doehner. The anima image on the cover: Bernardo Buontalenti, Ninfa marina, Firenze, B.N.F., C.B., 3, 53¹¹, c. 10r; Fotocolor G. Sansoni, per concessione della Bibl. Naz. Firenze and selected by Pierre Denivelle.

Mary Vernon acknowledges the following sources for assorted details of her images: Carol B. Grafton, *Treasury of Art Nouveau Design and Ornament*; Jim Harter, *Harter's Picture Archive*; Jim Harter, *Women: A Pictorial Archive from Nineteenth-Century Sources*; and Theodore Menten, *Pictorial Archive of Quaint Woodcuts: Joseph Crawhall*, all from Dover Publications.

Most of all, the author and publisher gratefully acknowledge the use of excerpts from the following volumes of *The Collected Works of C. G. Jung*, trans. R. F. C. Hull, Bollingen Series XX. The excerpts are reprinted with permission of Princeton University Press.

Vol. 5   *Symbols of Transformation*, copyright © 1956 by Princeton University Press.
Vol. 6   *Psychological Types*, copyright © 1971 by Princeton University Press.
Vol. 7   *Two Essays on Analytical Psychology*, copyright 1953, © 1966 by Princeton University Press.
Vol. 8   *The Structure and Dynamics of the Psyche*, copyright © 1960, 1969 by Princeton University Press.
Vol. 9   I, *The Archetypes and the Collective Unconscious*, copyright © 1959, 1969 by Princeton University Press.
Vol. 9   II, *Aion: Researches into the Phenomenology of the Self*, copyright © 1959 by Princeton University Press.
Vol. 10   *Civilization in Transition*, copyright © 1964, 1970 by Princeton University Press.
Vol. 11   *Psychology and Religion: West and East*, copyright © 1958, 1969 by Princeton University Press.
Vol. 12   *Psychology and Alchemy*, copyright 1953, © 1968 by Princeton University Press.
Vol. 13   *Alchemical Studies*, copyright © 1967 by Princeton University Press.
Vol. 14   *Mysterium Coniunctionis*, copyright © 1965, 1970 by Princeton University Press.
Vol. 15   *The Spirit in Man, Art, and Literature*, copyright © 1966 by Princeton University Press.
Vol. 16   *The Practice of Psychotherapy*, copyright 1954, © 1966 by Princeton University Press.
Vol. 17   *The Development of Personality*, copyright 1954 by Princeton University Press.
Vol. 18   *The Symbolic Life*, copyright 1950, 1953, copyright © 1955, 1958, 1959, 1963, 1968, 1969, 1970, 1973, 1976 by Princeton University Press.

The author and publisher also thank Routledge & Kegan Paul Ltd. (London), publisher of the above-mentioned edition of *The Collected Works of C. G. Jung* in Great Britain.

CONTENTS

Editorial Note

In the pages that follow, an essay by James Hillman appears on the righthand pages, while relevant quotations from the works of Carl Gustav Jung are printed to the left. Bold superscript letters in Hillman's essay refer the reader to the appropriate material, which may be one quote or several. These alphabetic letters start over again at "A" on every set of facing pages.

Hillman's introduction lists on page five the two abbreviations of Jung's works used to identify the quotations' sources. Readers unfamiliar with his *Collected Works* should know these are referred to by volume and paragraph numbers.

Excluding capitalization of initial letters, all of Spring Publications' editorial interpolations in Jung's material are indicated by bold brackets. Regular brackets are either reproduced from the original material or enclose Jung's material which has been transposed from one place to another in a given quote. An "N" in parentheses in a quote's reference shows that Spring has appended the relevant footnote from the *Collected Works*.

MHGS
1985

Preface

Here is an essay that can stand for itself. Usually after twelve years one wants to re-do the job. The urge to improve. Instead, I am amazed with the way it is – that it was done so thoroughly and that it was done at all. It needed only some re-formulations, extensions, and practical cautions – in twelve years one does learn a thing or two about anima. But once embarked on these expansions, I could barely contain them within these pages. What an instigator anima can be, though I doubt whether this essay, aimed at clarifying her notion in my mind, did much to untangle her effects in my life. Still today I defend myself against her with both idealizations and scepticism.

The essay began as an excursion that I felt was essential to the body of *Re-Visioning Psychology* (1975), but soon anima claimed more display than the proportions of that work would allow. The essay was even too flamboyant to print as one piece and so had to be cut into halves (*Spring 1973* and *Spring 1974*). Those issues of that annual are long out of print, which gives the efficient cause for making the essay into this book.

There are further causes, more deep-seated reasons. As I look back, it seems my work has always been anima-based, from *Emotion* (1960) to "Betrayal" and the Psyche/Eros tale as the myth of analysis, on to "soul-making," and more recently, the focus on the aesthetic imagination and the soul of the world (*anima mundi*). Specialized chapters of investigation into the salt, the silver, and the color blue in alchemy also elaborate upon anima phenomenology. If anima is my root metaphor, it seems psychologically necessary to delve into this component who dominates my thought, colors my style, and has so graciously proffered themes for my attention.

Moreover, isn't *devotio* to anima the calling of psychology? So, another deep-seated reason for this book is to provide grounding for the vision of soul in psychology, so that psychology doesn't abandon itself to the archetypal perspectives of the Child and developmentalism or the Mother and material causalism. The vision of soul given by anima is more than just one more perspective. The call of soul convinces; it is a seduction into psychological faith, a faith in images and the thought of the heart, into an animation of the world. Anima attaches and involves. She makes us fall into love. We cannot remain the detached observer looking through a lens. In fact, she probably doesn't partake in optical metaphors at all. Instead, she is continually weaving, stewing, and enchanting consciousness into passionate attachments away from the vantage point of a perspective.

The book could never have happened had not Gerald James Donat checked every single reference for probable inaccuracies – and there are some five hundred references to Jung in what follows. Mr. Donat raised many serious questions that had to be dealt with, and this text stands refined owing to his genius for detail and his powers of stubborn reasoning. Peter Bishop then copied the passages from Jung and set them *en face*, giving the book its basic form. Mr. Bishop was studious and exacting with his labor, and he carried it out beautifully. Then Joseph Cambray reviewed what had been done, carefully finishing up loose ends and adjusting my last-minute irrational insertions.

Finally, Mary Helen Gray Sullivan stepped in, copy-editing, checking the references again, matching passages that didn't match, inserting alterations and additions, designing the book page-by-page, discovering new queries – once again making me conscious of my failings. Though the book goes forth under one sole name, there are really four other authors – Mrs. Sullivan and the Messrs. Donat, Bishop, and Cambray. (The faults, however, are all mine.) And of course, a fifth, whose words, and whose anima, made the whole task worthwhile for us all – C. G. Jung.

I take the occasion also to thank Tree Swenson for giving so much good advice on the design of the book and to Princeton University Press and Routledge and Kegan Paul for permission to quote from the writings of C. G. Jung.

J.H.
1985

Take for instance *animus* and *anima*. No philosopher in his senses would invent such irrational and clumsy ideas.

C. G. JUNG, Letter to Calvin S. Hall

The ground principles, the *archai*, of the unconscious are indescribable because of their wealth of reference. . . . The discriminating intellect naturally keeps on trying to establish their singleness of meaning and thus misses the essential point; for what we can above all establish as the one thing consistent with their nature is their manifold meaning, their almost limitless wealth of reference, which makes any unilateral formulation impossible.

C. G. JUNG, CW 9, i, §80

I

... if a man does not know what a thing *is*, it is at least
an increase in knowledge if he knows what it is *not*.

C. G. JUNG
last phrase of *Aion*

Introduction

THIS excursion is intended to supplement the main literature
on the anima.[1] Since that literature provides a goodly phenomenology of the *experience* of anima, I shall look here more closely at
the rather neglected phenomenology of the *notion* of anima. Experience and notion affect each other reciprocally. Not only do we
derive our notions out of our experiences in accordance with the
fantasy of empiricism, but also our notions condition the nature of
our experiences. In particular there seems to me to be a sentimentalism suffusing "anima" which I suspect is embedded in the notion
itself, thereby coloring pale and pink our experiences and the
assessments of those experiences. So, examining our experiences
cannot rectify this sentimentalism, since they have already been
prejudged by the rose-tinted glasses given us, I suspect, by the notion. We do better looking into the notion, if that is where the sentimentalism lies. Of course, "anima" marks out a difficult region of
the psyche, hardly lending itself to any sort of examination. But
the difficulty we have with anima arises as much from our indistinct concepts of her as from her indistinct nature. Jung often ex-

(a) According to these Gnostics, . . . the feminine figure of Wisdom, [was] Sophia-Achamoth. . . . Sophia, partly by an act of reflection and partly driven by necessity, entered into relation with the outer darkness. The sufferings that befell her took the form of various emotions – sadness, fear, bewilderment, confusion, longing; now she laughed and now she wept. . . .

The emotional state of Sophia sunk in unconsciousness . . . , her formlessness, and the possibility of her getting lost in the darkness characterize very clearly the anima of a man who identifies himself absolutely with his reason and his spirituality.

CW 13, §452 ff.

(b) If the encounter with the shadow is the "apprentice-piece" in the individual's development, then that with the anima is the "master-piece."

CW 9, i, §61 (cf. 9 February 1959, Letter to Traugott Egloff)

(c) . . . I have noticed that people usually have not much difficulty in picturing to themselves what is meant by the shadow. . . . But it costs them enormous difficulties to understand what the anima is. They accept her easily enough when she appears in novels or as a film star, but she is not understood at all when it comes to seeing the role she plays in their own lives, because she sums up everything that a man can never get the better of and never finishes coping with. Therefore it remains in a perpetual state of emotionality which must not be touched. The degree of unconsciousness one meets with in this connection is, to put it mildly, astounding.

CW 9, i, §485

plained the therapeutic value of concepts as ways of taking hold, of grasping and comprehending, so that precise conceptual thinking and feeling, especially in regard to such a vague and subtle *fascinosum* as the anima, serve psychological consciousness.

It may be argued that the very uncertainty is appropriate to anima and that conceptual clarification is to use intellect where it does not belong. Our concepts reflect her best when they are vague. To me, this all-too-familiar argument means having embraced the anima foolishly and having been dragged by her into the woods. As we are supposed not to let her rule in the realm of personal relationship where, as Eve, she would make us all too fleshly and literal, so too we may not let her dominate the realm of ideation where, as Sophia, she would make us confused and formless.[a] We can as well be victims of anima projection with sentimental ideas that cloud and turn our heads as with persons. The *sacrificium intellectus* in analytical psychology today sometimes becomes perverted from its authentic meaning – dedicating intellect to the Gods – to abandoning the burden of it for tendermindedness and fuzz. Neither Freud nor Jung had to cut off his head in order to serve psyche. If Sophia is one face of anima, then a subtleness in the application of mind is surely no affront to her and may instead be one of her claims upon the psychologist and an exercise in which she delights.

Precision in regard to anima seems particularly relevant for two further reasons: first, because our society, and psychology as part of it, is in high tension concerning feeling, femininity, eros, soul, fantasy – all areas which analytical psychology has involved with anima; and second, because Jung has said that for the individual the *Auseinandersetzung* "with the anima is the 'master-piece'" of psychological work.[b] Again, clarification of what the notion carries may afford some insight into the social and the individual confusions, including mine, as I write, and yours, as you read.[c]

"Anima" receives several definitions in Jung. These can be taken as levels of distinction which we may separate before attempting to understand their inter-relation. By levels I do not want to imply a hierarchy of stages or grades of value but merely facets superimposed upon one another. These several definitions need not be treated historically, for we are not engaged in a study of the devel-

3

(a) . . . valuable reference to *Tristram Shandy* [1759–67]. ["the two souls in every man living, – the one . . . being called the ANIMUS, the other, the ANIMA" (London, 1911, p. 133).] To begin with I did not have the feeling at all that I was guilty of plagiarism with my [anima/animus] theory, but in the last 5 years . . . I have discovered . . . traces of it also in the old alchemists. . . . I can only think that Laurence Sterne drew upon the secret teachings (presumably Rosicrucian) of his time. They contain the Royal Secret of the King and Queen, who were none other than the animus and anima, or Deus and Dea.   8 December 1938, Letter to Georgette Boner

(b) No man is so entirely masculine that he has nothing feminine in him. . . . The repression of feminine traits . . . causes these contra-sexual demands to accumulate in the unconscious.

CW 7, §297 (cf. §§296–301)

. . . the feminine belongs to man as his own unconscious femininity, which I have called the anima.   CW 5, §678

It is normal for a man to resist his anima, because she represents . . . all those tendencies and contents hitherto excluded from conscious life.   CW 11, §129

opment of the anima concept in Jung's mind.[a] Rather, I would regard the notions phenomenologically, using the *Collected Works* (CW), and occasionally *Memories, Dreams, Reflections* (MDR) and Jung's *Letters* (referred to by date and recipient),[2] as a single corpus without special attention to the chronological order of the anima notions or their contexts.

1. Anima and Contrasexuality

JUNG and the literature of analytical psychology mainly employ "anima" to refer to the contrasexual, less conscious aspect of the psyche of men.[b] "The anima can be defined as the image or archetype or deposit of all the experiences of man with woman" (CW 13, §58). This basic definition, which places anima in the psyche of men only, is reinforced with a biological speculation: "The anima is presumably a psychic representation of the minority of female

(a) We might compare masculinity and femininity and their psychic components to a definite store of substances. . . .   CW 8, §782

Either sex is inhabited by the opposite sex up to a point, for, biologically speaking, it is simply the greater number of masculine genes that tips the scales in favour of masculinity. The smaller number of feminine genes seems to form a feminine character, which usually remains unconscious because of its subordinate position.   CW 9, i, §58

. . . sex is determined by a majority of male or female genes, as the case may be. But the minority of genes belonging to the other sex does not simply disappear. A man therefore has in him a feminine side, an unconscious feminine figure – a fact of which he is generally quite unaware. I may take it as known that I have called this figure the "anima". . . .   CW 9, i, §512

The anima, being psychologically the female counterpart of the masculine consciousness, based upon the minority of female genes in a masculine body . . .
                8 January 1948, Letter to Canon H. G. England

. . . every man "carries Eve, his wife, hidden in his body." It is this feminine element in every man (based on the minority of female genes in his biological make-up) which I have called the *anima*.
                CW 18, §429

(b) The fact that the rotundum is . . . contained in the anima and is prefigured by her lends her that extraordinary fascination. . . . At a certain level, therefore, woman appears as the true carrier of the longed-for wholeness and redemption.   CW 14, §500

Whenever this drive for wholeness appears, it begins by disguising itself under the symbolism of incest, for, unless he seeks it in himself, a man's nearest feminine counterpart is to be found in his mother, sister, or daughter.   CW 16, §471

genes in a man's body" (CW 11, §48).[a] Anima thus becomes the carrier and even the image of "wholeness,"[b] since she completes the hermaphrodite both psychologically and as representative of man's biological contrasexuality.

If anima represents man's female lacuna, then a therapy governed by the idea of individuation toward wholeness focuses mainly upon her development. Anima development has thus become a major therapeutic tenet in the minds of many analytical psychologists, and the "development of the feminine," a major plank in the platform of analytical psychology. But as long as "anima" remains a portmanteau idea packed thick with other notions – eros, feeling, human relationships, introversion, fantasy, concrete life, and others we shall be uncovering as we proceed – the development of anima, like anima herself, continues to mean many things to many men. In the guise of "anima development," there takes place a rich trade in smuggled hypotheses, pretty pieties about eros, and eschatological indulgences about saving one's soul through relationship, becoming more feminine, and the sacrifice of intellect.

(a) To the young boy a clearly discernible anima-form appears in his mother. . . . An infantile man generally has a maternal anima; an adult man, the figure of a younger woman. The senile man finds compensation in a very young girl, or even a child.

CW 9, i, §357

In both cases [anima and animus] the incest element plays an important part: there is a relation between the young woman and her father, the older woman and her son, the young man and his mother, the older man and his daughter. CW 16, §521

If she is old, this is an indication that one's consciousness has become considerably more childish. If she is young, then one is too old in one's conscious attitude. 22 March 1935, Letter to Dr. S.

(b) The feelings of a man are so to speak a woman's and appear as such in dreams. I designate this figure by the term *anima*, because she is the personification of the inferior functions which relate a man to the collective unconscious. CW 18, §187

(c) The inner personality is the way one behaves in relation to one's inner psychic processes; it is the inner attitude, the characteristic face, that is turned towards the unconscious. I call the outer attitude, the outward face, the *persona*; the inner attitude, the inward face, I call the *anima*. CW 6, §803

. . . in a man the soul, i.e., anima, or inner attitude, is represented in the unconscious by definite persons with the corresponding qualities. Such an image is called a "soul-image." Sometimes these images are of quite unknown or mythological figures.

CW 6, §808

The first notion of anima as the contrasexual side of man is conceived within a fantasy of opposites.[3] Men and women are opposites, conscious and unconscious are opposites, conscious masculinity and unconscious femininity are opposites. These oppositions are qualified further by others: a youthful consciousness has an elderly anima figure; an adult pairs with a *soror* image near his own age; senile consciousness finds correspondence in a girl child.[a] Then, too, a social factor enters into the contrasexual definition. In several passages[b] "anima" refers to the contrasocial, inferior personality. There is an opposition between the external role one plays in social life and the interior, less conscious life of the soul. This less conscious aspect which is turned inward and experienced as one's personal interiority is the anima as "soul-image."[c]

(a) When the anima continually thwarts the good intentions of the conscious mind, by contriving a private life that stands in sorry contrast to the dazzling persona, it is exactly the same as when a naïve individual, who has not the ghost of a persona, encounters the most painful difficulties in his passage through the world. . . . But if we reverse the picture and confront the man who possesses a brilliant persona with the anima, . . . then we shall see that the latter is just as well informed about the anima and her affairs as the former is about the world.   CW 7, §318

(b) We might compare masculinity and femininity and their psychic components to a definite store of substances of which, in the first half of life, unequal use is made. A man consumes his large supply of masculine substance and has left over only the smaller amount of feminine substance, which must now be put to use.

CW 8, §782

After the middle of life, however, permanent loss of the anima means a diminution of vitality, of flexibility, and of human kindness. The result, as a rule, is premature rigidity, crustiness, stereotypy, fanatical one-sidedness, obstinacy, pedantry, or else resignation, weariness, sloppiness, irresponsibility, and finally a childish *ramollissement* with a tendency to alcohol. After middle life, therefore, the connection with the archetypal sphere of experience should if possible be re-established.   CW 9, i, §147

The more a man identifies with his biological and social role as man (persona), the more will the anima dominate inwardly.[a] As the persona presides over adaptation to collective consciousness, so the anima rules the inner world of the collective unconscious. As male psychology, according to Jung,[b] shifts after mid-life toward its female opposite, so there is a physiological and social softening and weakening toward "the feminine," all of which are occasioned by the anima.

No doubt experience does confirm this first notion of the anima which holds her to be the inferior distaff side of men. Indeed, she is first encountered through the dream figures, emotions, symptomatic complaints, obsessive fantasies and projections of Western men. Anima is "the glamorous, possessive, moody, and sentimen-

(a) The anima . . . is the "energy of the heavy and the turbid"; it clings to the bodily, fleshly heart. Its effects are "sensuous desires and impulses to anger." "Whoever is sombre and moody on waking . . . is fettered to the anima." CW 13, §57

Take, for example, the "spotless" man of honour and public benefactor, whose tantrums and explosive moodiness terrify his wife and children. What is the anima doing here? CW 7, §319

(b) When the shadow, the inferior personality, is in large measure unconscious, the unconscious is represented by a masculine figure. CW 10, §714n21

(c) The growing youth must be able to free himself from the anima fascination of his mother. There are exceptions, notably artists, where the problem often takes a different turn; also homosexuality, which is usually characterized by identity with the anima. . . . Such a disposition should not be adjudged negative in all circumstances, in so far as it preserves the archetype of the Original Man, which a one-sided sexual being has, up to a point, lost. CW 9,i, §146

The homosexual relation between an older and a younger man can thus be of advantage to both sides and have a lasting value. An indispensable condition for the value of such a relation is the steadfastness of the friendship and their loyalty to it. But only too often this condition is lacking. . . . A friendship of this kind naturally involves a special cult of feeling, of the feminine element in a man. He becomes gushing, soulful, aesthetic, over-sensitive, etc. – in a word, effeminate. . . . CW 10, §220

tal seductress in a man" (CW 9, ii, §422). "She intensifies, exaggerates, falsifies, and mythologizes all emotional relations. . . ."[a]

However, the syndrome of inferior feminine traits in the personal sphere, like other syndromes (conversion hysteria or raving mania, for example), is relative to the dominants of the culture and the *Zeitgeist.* Syndromes current when Freud began psychoanalysis are less current today; the anima as a syndrome of excessive or inferior feminine traits is less evident as the culture moves toward incorporation of "typically anima" attitudes into its collective values. We should therefore not identify a *description* of the anima in a rigidly patriarchal, puritanically defensive, extravertedly willful and unsoulful period of history with her *definition.* Even if the anima exaggerates and mythologizes, her influence upon emotional relationships today when interiority of soul and contrasexuality are de rigueur will appear differently and be governed by other myths. The task now is to discover what descriptions suit her in this time and how she is mythologizing today.

Besides, quite independent of historical periods and their notions of effeminacy, there might be a sophisticated anima consciousness (in the troubadour, stage-actor, courtier, diplomat, painter, florist, decorator, or psychologist – although all these with a grain of salt) which refers less to unconscious femininity than to actual ego identity. A man may be mainly governed by anima without being unconscious, i.e., without showing undifferentiated or compulsive contrasexual traits. A man may indeed be quite a child of the anima in overt social behavior, living adaptedly in a collective consciousness that has again made room for what hitherto in this century would have been considered preposterously inferior anima subjectivity and feminine sensitivity. In face of these phenomena, analytical psychology is yet able to maintain its theory again by referring to the fantasy of opposites. This time "anima" is paired with the masculine shadow.[b] When a man's ego shows a preponderance of classical anima traits, then the unconscious is represented by the chthonic male shadow; when the ego in a man is feminine, then his unconscious contrasexuality must be masculine. Jung sometimes discusses male homosexuality as anima identification.[c]

Today the notions of "masculine" and "feminine" are in dispute. This dispute has helped differentiate gender roles from social ones,

(a) . . . it is essentially the overvaluation of the material object without that constellates a spiritual and immortal figure within (obviously for the purpose of compensation and self-regulation). . . . [A] compensatory relationship exists between persona and anima.

CW 7, §§303–04

Just as the persona is the image of himself which the subject presents to the world, and which is seen by the world, so the anima is the image of the subject in his relation to the collective unconscious. . . . One could also say: the anima is the face of the subject as seen by the collective unconscious. . . . If the ego adopts the standpoint of the anima, adaptation to reality is severely compromised.

CW 7, §521

. . . the character of the anima can be deduced from that of the persona. Everything that should normally be in the outer attitude, but is conspicuously absent, will invariably be found in the inner attitude. This is a fundamental rule. . . .

CW 6, §806

(b) As to the common human qualities, the character of the anima can be deduced from that of the persona. . . . But as regards its individual qualities, nothing can be deduced. . . . We can only be certain that when a man is identical with his persona, his individual qualities will be associated with the anima. This association frequently gives rise in dreams to the symbol of psychic pregnancy. . . . The child that is to be born signifies the individuality, which, though present, is not yet conscious.

CW 6, §806

and even to differentiate kinds of gender identity, i.e., whether based on primary or secondary, manifest or genetic, physical or psychic gender characteristics. It has become difficult to speak of the anima as inferior femininity since we are no longer certain just what we mean with "femininity," let alone "inferior" femininity. Moreover, archetypal psychology has placed the very notion of the ego in doubt.[4] Ego-identity is not just one thing, but in a polytheistic psychology "ego" reflects any of several archetypes and enacts various mythologems. It may as well be influenced by a Goddess as by a God or Hero, and it may as well display 'feminine' styles in behavior without this indicating either ego-weakness or incipient ego-loss. A man's ego may perform all the required functions of an ego without its being modeled upon Hercules or Christ. Neither captain, father, nor builder of cities, instead moving through the world as a child of Luna or of Venus, yet with all ego-functions of orientation, memory, association, and proprioception intact. We shall return to the ego/anima relation in chapters five and ten below.

Because the fantasy of opposites[a] keeps the anima in a social tandem with either the persona or the shadow and in a gender tandem with masculinity, we neglect her phenomenology per se and so find it difficult to understand her except in distinction to these other notions (masculinity, shadow, animus, persona). We are always regarding anima phenomenology from within a harness or from the opposite arm of a balance. Our notions are drawn in compensation to something else to which she is always yoked. (See below chapter ten on the Syzygy.) And, as the differences between social and sexual masculinity remain muddled, and our ideas of ego have hardened into dogmatic clichés, the anima's *definition* tends to be derivative of – and not demarcated enough from – her cultural and historical occasions. Yet, the *phenomenology* of anima existed before and continues to exist independently of the psychological framework into which she has been put. In other words, anima gives each of us a sense of an individualized soul, altogether apart from whatever she might compensate. But this individualized soul is merely an intimation. And just this latency, this pregnancy in her unknownness, ignites the compulsions toward her. Because she bears in her belly our individualized becoming, we are drawn into soul-making.[b]

[handwritten] Anima defined from cultural definitions of ego, persona as opposites. But she also "bears" the individuality of our souls.

15

(a) ... on a low level the anima is a caricature of the feminine
Eros. ... Eros is an interweaving. ... Eros is relatedness. ...

CW 13, §60

It [salt] represents the feminine principle of Eros, which brings
everything into relationship. ... [S]alt, as the soul or spark of the
anima mundi, is ... the daughter of the spiritus vegetativus of creation.

CW 14, §322

Apart from its lunar wetness and its terrestrial nature, the most
outstanding properties of salt are bitterness and wisdom. ... Salt,
as the carrier of this fateful alternative, is co-ordinated with the nature of woman.

CW 14, §330

Confirmation of our interpretation of salt as Eros (i.e., as a feeling
relationship) is found in the fact that the bitterness is the origin of
the *colours*. ...

CW 14, §333

... the anima corresponds to the maternal Eros.   CW 9, ii, §29

... man will be forced to develop his feminine side, to open his
eyes to the psyche and to Eros. It is a task he cannot avoid, unless
he prefers to go trailing after woman in a hopelessly boyish fashion, worshipping from afar but always in danger of being stowed
away in her pocket.

CW 10, §259 (cf. §§255–58)

The anima has an erotic, emotional character. ... Hence most of
what men say about feminine eroticism, and particularly about the
emotional life of women, is derived from their own anima projections and distorted accordingly.

CW 17, §338

2. *Anima and Eros*

THIS implies that, in trying to lay bare a definite idea of anima, we shall beware of whatever descriptive traits she currently bears. The first ones to be questioned are the erotic traits.[a] Erotic contents and feelings have become attached by the anima archetype, but do they belong necessarily to it?

Erotic contents become attached to anima

(a) The Latin words *animus*, 'spirit', and *anima*, 'soul', are the same as the Greek *anemos*, 'wind'. The other Greek word for 'wind', *pneuma,* also means 'spirit'. In Gothic we find the same word in *us-anan,* 'to breathe out', and in Latin it is *anhelare,* 'to pant'. In Old High German, *spiritus sanctus* was rendered by *atum,* 'breath'. In Arabic, 'wind' is *rih,* and *ruh* is 'soul, spirit'. The Greek word *psyche* has similar connections; it is related to *psychein,* 'to breathe', *psychos,* 'cool', *psychros,* 'cold, chill', and *physa,* 'bellows'. These connections show clearly how in Latin, Greek, and Arabic the names given to the soul are related to the notion of moving air, the "cold breath of the spirits."   CW 8, §664

For Heraclitus the soul at the highest level is fiery and dry, because ψυχή as such is closely akin to "cool breath" – ψύχειν means 'to breathe,' 'to blow'; ψυχρός and ψῦχος mean 'cold,' 'chill,' 'damp.'
CW 9, i, §55

. . . the soul . . . was visualized sensuously as a breath-body. . . .
CW 14, §748

(b) . . . another fact to which I have already alluded, [is] the characteristically historical aspect of the soul.   CW 7, §303

. . . the *historical* aspect of . . . anima figures.   CW 7, §299

With this anima, then, we plunge straight into the ancient world.
CW 12, §112 (cf. CW 7, §§299–303)

(c) If we examine their content, . . . we find countless archaic and "historical" associations. . . . They [the anima and animus] evidently live and function . . . especially in that phylogenetic substratum which I have called the collective unconscious. . . . [T]hey bring into our ephemeral consciousness an unknown psychic life belonging to a remote past. It is the mind of our unknown ancestors. . . .   CW 9, i, §518

Linguistically and phenomenologically, *anima* and *psyché*[5] have more to do with air, the living air of the head as a holy seat of generative power (later, our *anima rationalis* or intellectual soul), with breath as Jung points out,[a] with dew and heavy cool vapor, and even with earth and death (*p'o* soul, *anima telluris*) than with fire and desire.[6] This vaporous soul substance, like the mists that hang over marshes, the water-fowl, the hollow reeds and the breezes stirring the reeds, finds parallels in Bachofen ("hetaerism"), in Roscher's *Lexikon* ("nymphs"), in Emma Jung ("Naturwesen").[7] Elsewhere[8] I have set out some of the traditionally contrasting phenomenologies of anima and eros so that there is no need to resume them but briefly here. The first is moist, vegetative, receptive, indirect, ambiguous; its consciousness is reflective and in flux. The second is fiery, phallic, spirited, directed, sporadic and unattached, vertical as an arrow, torch, or ladder.

Anima "immediately surrounds herself with a peculiar historical feeling" (CW 10, §85).[9] There is a sense of history evoked especially by the anima archetype;[b] "She likes to appear in historic dress" (CW 9, i, §60), and she "has a peculiar relationship to *time*" (CW 9, i, §356). Her historical associations go down to the archaic, even phylogenetic, past.[c] Although animus may come through the father and be represented by a senex court of fathers and thus show equally strong conservatism, and even in "deepest essence" be "just as historically-minded as the anima" (CW 10, §89), nonetheless Jung makes one contrast between anima and animus in terms of a "mystical sense of history." Where anima reaches backward, animus is "more concerned with the present and the future" (ibid., §86). This distinction could be practically extrapolated: anima draws us into history, so that the struggle with history – of ourselves as cases, and of our ancestors and our culture – is a way of soul-making. The occupation with history, and the historical perspective, reflects anima. Occupation with the present in the political scene, social reform, comment on trends, and all futurology are animus – and this whether in men or women. Anima and animus need each other; for animus can make the past now relevant for the present and future, while anima gives depth and culture to current opinion and predictions. Without both together, we are either lost in archeological digs of academic anima-

19

(a) Four stages of eroticism were known in the late classical period: Hawwah (Eve), Helen (of Troy), the Virgin Mary, and Sophia. The series is repeated in Goethe's *Faust*: in the figures of Gretchen as the personification of a purely instinctual relationship (Eve); Helen as an anima figure; Mary as the personification of the "heavenly," i.e., Christian or religious, relationship; and the "eternal feminine" as an expression of the alchemical *Sapientia*. As the nomenclature shows, we are dealing with the heterosexual Eros or anima-figure in four stages, and consequently with four stages of the Eros cult. The first stage – Hawwah, Eve, earth – is purely biological; woman is equated with the mother and only represents something to be fertilized. The second stage is still dominated by the sexual Eros, but on an aesthetic and romantic level where woman has already acquired some value as an individual. The third stage raises Eros to the heights of religious devotion and thus spiritualizes him: Hawwah has been replaced by spiritual motherhood. Finally, the fourth stage illustrates something which unexpectedly goes beyond the almost unsurpassable third stage: *Sapientia*. . . . This stage represents a spiritualization of Helen and consequently of Eros as such. CW 16, §361

(b) "[*Anima*] is a subtle imperceptible smoke." CW 12, §394n105

refinement or riding the wave of the future, following animus into space-age science-fiction and pollution/population doom.

In contradistinction to the historical depth of anima, Eros is forever young, has no history and even wipes out history, or creates its own, its "love-story." And where anima withdraws toward meditative isolation – the retreat of the soul – eros seeks unions.

Even where Jung speaks of "four stages of eroticism"[a] and correlates the four stages of erotic phenomenology with four grades of the anima (Eve, Helen, Mary, Sophia), the feminine images are not the eros itself but the objects of its longing (pothos). A drive has a corresponding projection, a goal it seeks, a grail to hold its blood. These containers may be represented by the anima images which Jung describes, and a quality of eros may be correlated with each of these figures, but the figures are not the eros. They are not the lovers but the beloveds; they are reflections of love. They are the means by which eros can see itself. When our desire is mirrored by a cheering coed or a nursing nun, through the specificity of the soul-image we are able to know more precisely about the quality of our desire. But the desire is not the cheerleader, not the nurse. The images are soul-portraits by means of which eros is drawn into the psychic field and can be witnessed as a psychic event.

Bachelard[10] associates anima with reverie (in contradistinction to animus and the activity of dreaming); Corbin[11] with imagination; Ficino[12] with fantasy (idolum) and fate; Onians[13] with life and death; Porphyry[14] with a damp spirit and "aerial opacity."[15,b] These traditional phenomenologies of the notion of soul, including the lengthy lunar descriptions of anima in Jung (CW 14, §§154–233), do not have markedly erotic traits. These notions do not identify anima with eros or attribute the eros principle to soul. Moreover, where anima has classically referred to an internally located function in deepest association with human life and its fate, eros is a daimon, external, that visits itself upon life and fate. We fall in and out of love or are carried and redeemed, or cursed, through its working, but that which love works upon is not love but soul. Soul is the arrow's target, the fire's combustible material, the labyrinth through which it dances. It is especially this structural notion that I would emphasize: anima as an *archetypal structure of consciousness*. As such it provides a specifically structured

21

mode of being in the world, a way of behaving, perceiving, feeling that gives events the significance not of love but of soul. Now, what more can we say about this structure? What are its differentiating features, if they are not erotic?

Anima is inward (hence "closed" and called "virginal" in religious and poetic metaphors of the soul), devoted, yet labile, generous and generative, yet reserved (shy, shameful, retreating, pure, veiled – these latter qualities presented by the virgin nymphs and Goddesses such as Maria or Artemis). To this interiority belongs a movement of deepening downward[16] (caves, deeps, graves) which in the phenomenology of Kore–Persephone connects her with the realm of the underworld. "*Anima* was not the usual name for the life-soul till after death."[17] She carries our death; our death is lodged in the soul. Again, these notions are far from any thought of the anima as the eros principle, especially where eros has come to mean – and not only through Freud – the libido, the life-impulse opposed to death.

This consciousness is mood-determined, a notion that has been represented in mythological phenomenology by images of natural atmospheres (clouds, waves, still waters). Anima-consciousness favors a protective mimicry, an *attachment* to something or someone else to which it is echo. Here we see the wood nymphs that belong to trees, the souls which hover over waters, speak from dells and caves, or sing from sea-rocks and whirlpools – and, most vividly, the succubus. That we conceive anima in tandems is already given by her phenomenology. So, we think of her in notions of attachment with body or with spirit, or in the mother–daughter mystery, in the masculine–feminine pairings, or in compensation with the persona, in collusion with the shadow, or as guide to the self.

In these pairs, like in the mythological imagery, anima is the reflective partner; she it is who provides the moment of reflection in the midst of what is naturally given. She is the psychic factor in nature, an idea formulated in the last century as "animism." We feel this moment of reflection in the contrary emotions that anima phenomena constellate: the fascination plus danger, the awe plus desire, the submission to her as fate plus suspicion, the intense awareness that this way lie both my life and my death. Without these soul-stirring emotions, there would be no significance in the

(a) But how do we dare to call this elfin being the "anima"? Anima means soul and should designate something very wonderful and immortal. Yet this was not always so. We should not forget that this kind of soul is a dogmatic conception whose purpose it is to pin down and capture something uncannily alive and active. The German word *Seele* is closely related, via the Gothic form *saiwalô*, to the Greek word αἰόλος , which means 'quick-moving,' 'changeful of hue,' 'twinkling,' something like a butterfly – ψυχή in Greek – which reels drunkenly from flower to flower and lives on honey and love.   CW 9,i, §55

. . . the soul, that glancing, Aeolian thing, elusive as a butterfly (anima, ψυχή).   CW 9,i, §391

(b) Hermes, originally a wind god, and his counterpart the Egyptian Thoth, who "makes the souls to breathe," are the forerunners of the alchemical Mercurius in his aerial aspect. The texts often use the terms *pneuma* and *spiritus* in the original concrete sense of "air in motion." . . . He is the . . . stone uplifted by the wind. . . .

"Soul" represents a higher concept than "spirit" in the sense of air or gas. As the "subtle body" or "breath-soul" it means something non-material and finer than mere air. Its essential characteristic is to animate and be animated. . . . Mercurius is often designated as *anima*. . . .   CW 13, §§261–62

. . . the *anima iliastri* can burst forth from the heart when it lacks "air"; that is to say, if psychic remedies are not applied, death occurs prematurely.   CW 13, §201

natural places and human affairs to which she is attached. But, life, fate, and death cannot become 'conscious,' so that with her is constellated a consciousness of our fundamental unconsciousness. In other words, consciousness of this archetypal structure is never far from unconsciousness. Its primary attachment is to the state of nature, to all things that simply are – life, fate, death – and which can only be reflected but never separated from their impenetrable opacity. Anima stays close to this field of the natural unconscious mind.

A consciousness that does not soar but stays attached, that hovers and flutters over the field of natural events, is imaged also by the butterfly.[a] The fascination of moth for flame has long stood for the soul's fluttering attachment to eros, and the butterfly sucking its sustenance from the flowers of feeling again has represented the psyche–eros relation. The butterfly points again to air as the psyche's element. To be in the air, put on airs, be breezy, windy, breathless, or show shifts of atmospheric pressure all belong to anima.[b] Low-flying in dreams, especially over furniture or persons in rooms (closed, interior, within), can be distinguished from puer-soaring and is not necessarily a dangerous sign of "having no earth," of inflation, of being out of the body. I take this flying as part of anima phenomenology and air as a legitimate element for certain conditions of the soul. Low-flying in childhood dreams I take as a possible announcement of anima consciousness.

Like the butterfly, anima-consciousness moves through phases, bearing a process, a history. It is egg, worm, cocoon, bright wing – and not only successively but all at once. Our strongly evolutional approach to events and images makes us always see development first, forgetting that in the realm of the imaginal all processes that belong to an image are inherent to it at all times. There is not merely a *coincidentia oppositorum* but a coincidence of processes. All phases at once: no first and last, better and worse, progression and regression. Instead, soul history as a series of images, superimposed. The tale of their interaction the Mother would turn into growth, the Child into futurity, and the Hero into an evolutionary epic of achievement. Because our consciousness is in thrall to these archetypal structures, we are unable to envision a phenomenology of phases except as development, as if the butterfly were a moral pilgrim. But the choice of an image from nature does not imply the

25

(a) The whore (*meretrix*) is a well-known figure in alchemy. She characterizes the arcane substance in its initial, "chaotic," maternal state. . . . "That noble whore Venus. . . ."　　　　CW 14, §415

(b) Everything the anima touches becomes numinous – unconditional, dangerous, taboo, magical.　　　　CW 9, i, §59

(c) . . . the anima is bipolar and can therefore appear positive one moment and negative the next; now young, now old; now mother, now maiden; now a good fairy, now a witch; now a saint, now a whore.　　　　CW 9, i, §356

(d) . . . Michael Maier's journey to the seven mouths of the Nile, which signify the seven planets. . . . is a description of the dreamer's ascent to a world of gods and heroes, of his initiation into a Venus mystery. . . .

. . . Our author was led in the first place by the anima-sibyl to undertake the journey through the planetary houses. . . .

CW 14, §297 f.

naturalistic fallacy in regard to its interpretation. *Psyché* as butter-fly does not demand that we view the soul developmentally.

Despite these distinctions between eros and psyche and a char-acterization of psyche apart from eros, there remain of course the ladies of pleasure who pay their sensuous call in our dreams. They seem erotic in themselves, thus giving phenomenological ground to the notion of anima as eros.

Here I believe we do well to remember that all that is female is not necessarily anima and that all that is anima is not necessarily Venusian. Venus phenomenology in dream and fantasy becomes ennobled by the word 'soul,' which both overloads the aphrodisiac facet of the psyche and also undervalues Venus in her own right. The whore in a dream is a whore, who can take on deeper psychological significance (cf. the "great whore" [*meretrix*] in al-chemy)[a] as an archetypal image in her own right and need not be the anima, my mistress soul, psychopomp to the self, that is, un-less she be *numinous*[b] and carry all the fascinating bipolar perplex-ities by which the anima archetype is recognized[c] – old and young, frail and physical, culture and nature, innocent and vile, intimate and occult. We do injustice to the complexity of anima by calling every woman streetwalking through our dreams an 'anima image'; and we neglect Aphrodite as an authentic structure of con-sciousness when we psychologize her into an 'anima figure.'

To take seriously Aphrodite's archetypal realm and its patterns of behavior means to take them *as such* without conflating, and in-flating, them with the import of soul. The seductive Venusian fig-ures draw me into the realm of Venus as Ulysses went to Calypso and to Circe or as Michael Maier journeys into the planetary hous-es.[d] But neither in the *Odyssey* nor in Maier's alchemy does Venus stand for soul. Ulysses has as guide Athene, and Maier's psycho-pompos is a sibyl – soul as psychological understanding rather than as eros. There is evidently more to soul than Venus, and more to Venus than soul.

On the one hand, giving soul to each chick and duck and silly goose that enters fantasy loads these images and the human rela-tionships in which they appear with disproportionate significance. When analysts put soul values onto simply Venusian affairs, they serve her as couplers, even while burdening the pleasures of life with 'anima development.'

27

[margin handwritten note: aphrodite is not the anima]

(a) Of course, I did not invent the term Eros. I learnt it from Plato. But I never would have applied this term if I hadn't observed facts that gave me a hint how to use this Platonic notion. With Plato Eros is still a daimonion or daemonium. . . .

18 June 1947, Letter to Ermine Huntress Lantero

(b) Four stages of eroticism were known in the late classical period. . . . The series is repeated in Goethe's *Faust*: in the figures of Gretchen as the personification of a purely instinctual relationship (Eve); Helen as an anima figure; Mary as the personification of the "heavenly" . . . ; and the "eternal feminine" as an expression of the alchemical *Sapientia*. CW 16, §361

On the other hand, Venus is one of the way-stations, and she must get her due. Modern man has an accumulated debt to Aphrodite on which she is today exacting payments at a furious rate. It is as if she were actually demanding our souls for all the centuries that they were denied to her by Judeo-Christian repression. But we pay her back best in the true coin of Aphrodite. To pay her in the guise of soul-indulgences cheats the real cost. It is more comforting to visit her planetary house in the name of anima development than it is to suffer the venereal evils, entanglements, perversions, revenges, furies, and soporific pleasures for her sake alone.

The contemporary analytical confusion of soul with eros has its source, I believe, in the archetypal perspective of Aphrodite. She would insist that we look at phenomena through the eyes of Eros, her son. By maintaining this perspective she would be perpetually reclaiming this son to serve a Venusian and venereal view of soul and of femininity. She above all has an interest in keeping Eros on the feminine side of the coniunctio. If Eros is kept on her side, his eroticism will be stimulated in an aphrodisiac fashion, giving that cast to eros in our consciousness today in which it is so highly sexualized. Socratic/Platonic Eros – from where Jung says he took the expression[a] – is definitely masculine. This Eros had Hermes in his genealogy, and so it has further aims than the Eros of Aphrodite which was for Socrates only one phase of erotic activity.

But Aphrodite still awaits recognition for the influence she has upon analytical psychology's notion of anima. The realm of anima often seems nothing other than Aphrodite's realm, erotic relationships, or as they are transmuted into Helen's, who was imagined in antiquity as Aphrodite's incarnation. There we supposedly find anima and there we develop it. (So much does Helen-Aphrodite color our notion that, when Jung writes of the four stages of eroticism,[b] it is to Helen in particular that he gives the qualification "anima figure.")

The paradigm of this erotic exercise is transference which in both Freud and Jung receives primarily an Aphroditic cast. This was so from the beginning in Paris at Charcot's clinic. Jung soon recognized the influence of Paris and Vienna upon the formulation of psychic events, and, in separating out the school of Zürich (a city where Venus is less at home), he first focused upon the libido

29

(a) Green, the life-colour, suits her [the anima] very well. . . .

CW 5, §678

The colour green . . . is associated with Venus.   CW 14, §393

(b) As regards the psychology of this picture, we must stress above all else that it depicts a human encounter where love plays the decisive part.   CW 16, §419

As to the frank eroticism of the pictures, . . . they have a symbolical rather than a pornographic meaning.   CW 16, §460

concept, renaming it psychic energy. With Jung's de-libidinizing the very basis of psychoanalytic theory, the archetypal premise of the unconscious shifted from Aphrodite to Hermes-Mercurius, and the soul's fluxions were removed from the sexual eroticism and personal concretism of Aphrodite.

But still she influences our notions. How we welcome her color green in fantasy and dreams,[a] indicating to what extent Venus has colored our view of psychic events. They are seen through the green lenses of her world, growth, nature, life, and love, so that individuation tends to mean increasing beauty and harmony of soul. Little wonder that contemporary psychotherapeutic work – encounter, sensitivity, gestalt, Reichean – has led finally into overt demonstrations of Aphrodite: non-verbal, nakedness, feel-and-touch, body awareness, orgasm.

We may know a good deal about the manifestations of Aphrodite in myth and in our personal lives. But we know far too little about how she governs the premises and conclusions of our thinking. These we naively think are based on empirical facts. But the very idea of concrete, sensate facts suits her style of consciousness. The erotic 'facts' on which we build our ideas are her creations. Psychological evidence is never simply objective givens, lying around like moonrocks, waiting to be picked up. Empirical evidence of any psychological premise forms part of the same archetypal perspective: we find what we are looking for; we see what is allowed to fit in by the perceptual defenses in the archetypal structure of our consciousness. So we see the soul filled with sexual wishes when our premises and observations are Aphroditic. The Aphroditic cast of the anima in Jung's essay on transference is an excellent case in point.[b]

Aphrodite may have given the correct perspective to transference and may have been the gateway to the repressed (in our culture between 1870 and 1960), but it is not the anima's only, or even main, perspective. Athene, Artemis, Hera, and Persephone produce ideas of soul that would show another twist. To place anima events upon the altar of Aphrodite puts Psyche back in her service, back to the beginning of Apuleius's tale, the rest of which, and the very point of which, displays a movement away from Aphrodite, both of Eros and of Psyche.

If anima is defined as the eros factor, then we are always bound

31

(a) The unknown woman or anima [in dreams] always represents the "inferior," i.e., the undifferentiated function, which in the case of our dreamer is feeling.   CW 12, §150

Intellect and feeling . . . conflict with one another by definition. Whoever identifies with an intellectual standpoint will occasionally find his feeling confronting him like an enemy in the guise of the anima. . . .   CW 9, ii, §58

The feelings of a man are so to speak a woman's and appear as such in dreams. I designate this figure by the term *anima*. . . .
CW 18, §187

This spiritual inflation is compensated by a distinct inferiority of feeling, a real *undernourishment* of your other side, the feminine earth (*Yin*) side, that of personal feeling.
25 August 1928, Letter to Count Hermann Keyserling

to assume that sexual excitation is a soul message and cannot be denied – who would deny the call of his soul? And we are bound to assume that active human relationships and uplifting enthusiasms are anima-inspired, whereas in truth they are less promoted by the reflective moisture of the soul than by eros captivating the soul. For here we must concede that, though anima is not eros, her first inclination is toward love. So she seduces in order to be turned on, set afire, illumined. So she makes advances in order to move pure reflection into connection. So she commands an incredible range of voluptuous imagery in order to draw eros down upon her for what Plato called "generation," or soul-making. Nevertheless, though love be essential to soul, as theology insists and psychotherapy confirms, and though soul be that by which we receive love, soul is not love.

By drawing them apart in contrasts of moisture and fire, serpent and hare, waterfowl and dove, reflection and desire, fantasy and impulse, nature and spirit, mind and activity, depths and ascent, I am following the alchemists' dictum that only what has been properly separated can be adequately joined.

3. Anima and Feeling[18]

BESIDES eros, feeling too has been generally attributed to anima, as if she were the archetype of the feeling function. This confusion has several roots. The first and simplest lies in the idea of inferiority. When the feeling function in men is inferior (as is generally claimed by analytical psychology), it merges with men's contrasexual anima inferiority.[a] Then we believe we discriminate the anima *by* discriminating feeling, whereas the task more likely is one of discriminating anima *from* feeling, from the human related-

33

(a) The most striking feature about the anima-type is that the maternal element is entirely lacking. She is the companion and friend in her favourable aspect, in her unfavourable aspect she is the courtesan. . . . But the anima-type is presented in the most succinct and pregnant form in the Gnostic legend of Simon Magus. . . . [who] was always accompanied on his travels by a girl, whose name was Helen. He had found her in a brothel in Tyre; she was a reincarnation of Helen of Troy.   CW 10, §75

. . . Helen as an anima figure. . . .   CW 16, §361

Now comes the first transformation: he [Goethe] discovers his countertype ("feeling is all") and at the same time realizes the projection of the anima. . . . Behind Gretchen stands the Gnostic sequence: Helen-Mary-Sophia.
                                        22 March 1939, Letter to Anonymous

(b) It is principally among women that I have found the predominance of introverted feeling.   CW 6, §640

Feeling is a specifically feminine virtue. . . .   CW 10, §79

ness and personal evaluations that feeling has come to mean and which confine anima into the personal feeling world of Helen.[a]

Another source of the confusion between anima and feeling lies in an idea, only occasionally occurring in Jung[b] but bruited widely by later analytical psychologists, that feeling is a feminine prerogative. (Women are more at home in the feeling world; men learn about feeling from women; the development of the feminine goes by way of the feeling function.) Since anima is by definition feminine, then feeling refers to anima. Next in these steps of spurious reasoning erected on questionable premises is the equation: anima development = feeling development. Behind this equation still lurks the idea of eros, which is supposed to be the force within both the anima and the feeling function.

Just as anima is not eros or its psychic representative, so too the relation between the God-daimon Eros and eros as an archetypal principle, on the one hand, and feeling as a psychological function, on the other hand, has never been established – neither empirically, nor logically, nor phenomenologically. The feeling function works mainly through the realm of feeling of which at least fifteen hundred different ones have been named by psychology. Only some of this feeling has to do with eros. To give to eros either feeling or the anima puts too many events all upon one altar, claiming all for love. Not only is this biasedly Christian – in the sense of limited to only the one perspective of love – but also authentic aspects of anima become judged only from the standpoint of love. Hatred, spite, suspicion, jealousy, rejection, enmity, deception, betrayal, cruelty, misanthropy, ridicule play their part in anima experiences.

(a) The nixie is . . . a magical feminine being whom I call the *anima*. She can also be a siren, *melusina* (mermaid), wood-nymph, Grace, or Erlking's daughter, or a lamia or succubus, who infatuates young men and sucks the life out of them. . . .

   . . . An alluring nixie . . . is today called an "erotic fantasy," and she may complicate our psychic life in a most painful way. She comes upon us just as a nixie might; she sits on top of us like a succubus; she changes into all sorts of shapes like a witch. . . . [and] causes states of fascination that rival the best bewitchment. . . . She is a mischievous being who crosses our path in numerous transformations and disguises, playing all kinds of tricks on us, causing happy and unhappy delusions, depressions and ecstasies, outbursts of affect, etc. . . . the nixie has not laid aside her roguery. The witch has not ceased to mix her vile potions of love and death; her magic poison has been refined into intrigue and self-deception, unseen though none the less dangerous for that.

CW 9,i, §§53–54

(b) . . . the anima becomes, through integration, the Eros of consciousness, . . . the anima gives relationship and relatedness to a man's consciousness. . . . CW 9,ii, §33

In the case of the individual, the problem constellated by the shadow is answered on the plane of the anima, that is, through relatedness. CW 9,i, §487

. . . to the degree in which the shadow is recognized and integrated, the problem of the anima, i.e., of relationship, is constellated.

CW 9,i, §485n18

"She" [the anima] consists essentially in a certain inferior kind of relatedness to the surroundings and particularly to women. . . .

CW 18, §429

. . . the anima of a man consists of inferior relatedness, full of affect. . . . CW 13, §60

These emotions are appropriate to many of the cold-blooded, witchy creatures whom we find in legend and poetry[a] – and our dreams and lives – even where such "negative" emotions are far from the eros and the feeling function that would conform with the mediocre niceness of Christian humanism.

Yet another source lies in the idea of relationship. Jung (as we shall explore in chapter seven) often calls the anima the function of relationship. He also sometimes does consider anima to be that factor which can give "relationship and relatedness to a man's consciousness."[b] Although Jung himself only rarely describes feeling

(**a**) It often happens that the patient is quite satisfied with merely registering a dream or fantasy. . . . Others try to understand with their brains only. . . . That they should also have a *feeling-relationship* to the contents of the unconscious seems strange to them. . . .

CW 16, §489

as relatedness,[a] but rather feeling as valuation, analytical psychology now tends to stress the relational aspect. Feeling is generally spoken of as the instrument of connection between persons and between an individual and his outer and inner worlds. To have 'poor feeling' and to be 'unrelated' have become synonymous. Because both anima and feeling are called the function of relationship, they merge with each other.

Now, the two meanings of relationship, that of anima and that of feeling, touch each other only here and there. Yet today in some analytical psychology they have tended to fuse completely, so that anima = relationship = feeling has become the simple formula, nay, panacea. Before we swallow any more of this sweet elixir, or prescribe it to our patients, let us look at its ingredients.

Anima as relationship means that configuration which mediates between personal and collective, between actualities and beyond, between the individual conscious horizon and the primordial realm of the imaginal, its images, ideas, figures, and emotions. Here anima functions as mediatrix and psychopompos (see chapter seven below). The quality of relationship will be determined by this function. So, relationship governed by anima will show unstable paradoxes of longing and trepidation, involvement and skittishness, faith and doubt, and an intense sense of personal significance owing to the importance of the imaginal soul at large. The other main characteristic here, besides the emotional paradoxes and swollen importance, is the uncanny autonomy – the basic unconsciousness – of anima relationship because such relationship reflects her as bridge to everything unknown.

Anima as function of relationship is far indeed from relatedness. It seems odd that anima could ever have been considered as a help in human relationship. In each of her classical shapes she is a non-human or half-human creature, and her effects lead us away from the individually human situation. She makes moods, distortions, illusions, which serve human relatedness only where the persons concerned share the same mood or fantasy. If we want 'to relate,' then anima begone! Nothing disturbs more the accurate feeling between persons than anima. Even when her supposedly higher forms (Diotima, Aphrodite-Urania, Maria, Sophia) enter a relationship, a queenly atmosphere oppresses, and her psychopompos role is overshadowed with psychic pomposity.

Feeling as relationship is another kettle of fish. It refers to that function which brings object and subject into an evaluative *relatedness*. I size you up; or an event is discriminated by my scale of values into a particular shape ('feel') so that I recognize its importance relative to other events. "Relationship" here refers to a relatively constant process of assessment and valuation going on between consciousness and its content. By means of this process a relationship is established between consciousness and this content and among the contents themselves. (Thinking, also a rational function, provides relationship as well. It too discriminates, orders, and makes coherent connections among contents and between subject and object. Of course, it thinks these relationships in accordance with principles of thought, rather than feels them as values.)

The relatedness of George and Mary depends upon the specific natures of George and Mary. Their relatedness reflects their living process of feeling, and their relationship is unique to them. If their relationship were anima-determined, it would become a reflection less of them and more of an archetypal fantasy playing through them. Then they become collective actors performing an unconscious fantasy, i.e., lovers, quarrelers, cohorts, mother–son, father–daughter, nurse–patient, etc. Even the feeling function is usurped by the dominant fantasy. Then the specific complexity of the relatedness between George and Mary has become upstaged by an archetypal drama directed by the anima. Her purpose? To insist that the human respect her wider, more fateful kind of inhuman relatedness to impersonal factors that are archetypally prior even to human feeling.

One impersonal factor is culture. We have already seen that anima "surrounds herself with a peculiar historical feeling" (CW 10, §85). Her embeddedness in the history of a culture shapes human feeling in conformity with ethnic values and national manners (Jung's "racial" unconscious – CW 7, §434). Holding-hands and reciting poems among Arab youths are (or were) expressions of affection as correct as fighting among the Irish and keeping to oneself among Nordics. Culture determines even Jung's definition of the feeling function (CW 6, §723), for Jung refers mainly to late nineteenth-century German writers for his notion of it. Moreover, the authorities, whom he analyzes for determining his larger the-

ory of typology, are mainly Goethe, Nietzsche, Schiller, Spitteler, Lipps, Worringer, Gross, etc. "Gefühl ist alles," said Goethe in regard to Faust's encounter with Gretchen, and perhaps this was a Germanic anima speaking through him and then to Jung and now to us, blurring distinctions between feeling and anima.

If Jung's psychology reflects a Germanic anima, specifically it is Germanic Romantic. Ellenberger lists several major characteristics of Romanticism as they bear upon modern depth psychology.[19] All appear again and again in Jung's notion of anima as well as being basic to his psychology. First, "deep feeling for nature" and "speculations of the philosophy of nature." (Emma Jung entitled her paper on anima *Naturwesen*.) Second, penetration to the *Grund* which lies in the emotional soul (rather than reason), manifested best in universal symbols, parapsychology, dreams, and madness. Third, "the feeling for 'becoming'.... (which C. G. Jung was later to call individuation)" and "a strong emphasis upon the notion of the individual" whose perfectability is aided by the passions of love. Fourth, empathic feeling into other cultures and their differences, available through the study of myths, folktales, etc. Fifth, "a new feeling for history," especially the Middle Ages (the period of alchemy and Christian theology). According to Ellenberger,[20] even the term *anima* was partly influenced by the Romantic historian and mythologist Bachofen of Basel.[21]

By this turn to cultural history, I do not mean to reduce anima, or Jung, to Romanticism. I want only to show the influence of that specific anima, called Romantic, upon Jung's entire enterprise. For this enterprise is less concerned with society and family, science and technology, city and politics, reason and wit, classics and arts which an anima less romantic might well have inspired.

If anima is a cultural factor that shapes personal expression, then work on anima does re-work the feeling function at its roots. This helps to understand why changes in feeling are so slow: simply 'to relate' in a different style requires changes in our ancestors' modes and values, our culture's habits and tastes. We are working at the roots, *racines,* race. Those unchanging residues after conversion (Protestant to Catholic and vice versa), the adjustment snarls in interracial marriages, the culture shock after emigration from South to North (and v.v.) – these obduracies of feeling refer more deeply to matters of soul, to anima as conservative ancestress

43

who roots our human feeling in her historical soil. And, when human feeling departs at death and we join our ancestors, anima as the *p'o* soul (see below, chapter four) is reabsorbed into the cultural earth of one's racial geography perhaps only slightly affected by whatever courageous development of feeling has been achieved by an individual personality.

Yet when we look at Jung's drawings in the Red Book and the first incursion of anima in his active imaginations as described in his memoirs, it was neither Gretchen nor any Alpine or Rheinisch *Magd* who appeared to him, but blind Salome, a pathologized companion of a Gnostic sage (see below, chapter nine).

That is: there seems to be another impersonal factor in anima which is individual, endogenous, and independent of the racial unconscious. She and her companions brought Jung an individual fate and perhaps also a style of feeling. I mean by this his range of *Einfühlung* across cultures, his ability to distance by relating impersonally through ancient symbols, his fascination with and understanding of pathology, and, accompanying his wisdom, the blindness of which he has been accused in crucial relations, evaluations, and judgments (Helene, Sabina, Freud, National Socialism, and his choice of pupils).

The appreciation of Jung's feeling and his contribution to the psychology of feeling as a function must start with anima as an ancestrally ethnic dominant on the one hand, and, on the other, as an individually fateful constellation. Neither aspect, however, is human. Precisely this inhuman quality is her gift to feeling. *[margin handwriting: ethnically + individually affective]*

The muddling of anima and feeling contributes to that primrose path in analytical psychotherapy which considers the cure of souls to be an anima cultivation of a specific kind, i.e., feeling development. But anima cultivation, or soul-making to use the wider idea, is first of all a complex process of fantasying and understanding of which only part is the sophistication of feeling. Besides, the feeling that is developed through soul-making is perhaps more impersonal, a detailed sensitivity to the specific worth of psychic contents and attitudes, than it is personal. This development does *not* proceed from the impersonal to the personal, related, and human. Rather, the movement goes from the narrower embrace of my empirical human world and its personal concerns toward archetypal events that put my empirical, personal world in a more significant

frame. This frame is given, not by feeling or relatedness, but by the anima whose mythologizing fantasy and reflective function remind of life, fate, and death. She does not lead into human feeling but out of it. As the function that relates conscious and unconscious, she occludes conscious feeling, making it unconscious and making the human, inhuman. She puts other things in mind than the human world. But should Dante and Petrarch today go into psychotherapy, would they not be told that Beatrice and Laura were immature anima projections, unreal, regressive, revealing inferiority of feeling and unrelatedness to woman and 'the feminine'?

I, for one, have yet to be given convincing demonstration that in dreams a lizard requires development into something warm-blooded and a hyena into something more kindly, or that a little girl calls for development into mature feelings, and an uncanny witch-like woman or one impoverished or primitive is to be upgraded into the human world through feeling and personal relationships.

In these instances, ironically, maybe even tragically, the actual (anima?) images of lizard, little girl, and primitive slattern are not given feelings or evaluated with feeling for themselves as they are. Rather, in the name of feeling/anima development the actual image is depotentiated. All the feeling goes to the development, to the transformational progress of the images into something more human. It is as if the Christian myth of incarnation is continually being applied to the images of the anima, that all images must follow the model of the inhuman becoming human (incarnating), and that all psychic factors are to enter human relationships. Ridiculous, of course. Yet, putting anima development into the path of feeling development, as feeling is now humanistically understood, means precisely the slaying of the animals, the *daimones,* and the Gods. It means turning the sacred *numinosum* of an archetypal image into something safe, sane, and secular. Analytical psychotherapy, so bent upon humanizing the images and developing archetypal realities into relationships, is not only caught in Darwinism but also in the simplest sort of secularism where man is the measure and the Gods aberrations. But did not the Gods always have an aberrant and distorted aspect; were they not always strange forms in animal shapes, grotesque, bizarre, awe-full? Who says they must have warm blood or have human blood at all.

The dream child and the anima child (an anima-girl from child-

(a) We think we can congratulate ourselves on having already reached
     such a pinnacle of clarity, imagining that we have left all these
     phantasmal gods far behind. But what we have left behind are only
     verbal spectres, not the psychic facts that were responsible for the
     birth of the gods. We are still as much possessed by autonomous
     psychic contents as if they were Olympians. Today they are called
     phobias, obsessions, and so forth; in a word, neurotic symptoms.
     The gods have become diseases. . . .   CW 13, §54

hood, the thought of whom can still catch one's breath) do not necessarily signify undeveloped feelings. They may also be the gateways to the elfin world, or they may awaken nostalgic *pothos*, that yearning for intimacy with 'earlier' times and the first home. The archetypal child whom mythologists, and Jung, call Divine leaves its radiance on every undeveloped trait. Hence these traits are so difficult to renounce in the name of maturity. This peculiar radiance pulls us not only regressively to the childish and inferior, for it is also childlike and superb. We must be careful how we touch the 'immature.' Development as adaptive normalcy to the real world can be psychic child abuse, resulting in an imagination without access to its Real world.

To read the psyche's inhuman images as signals for feeling development leads right into the "humanistic fallacy," the belief that psyche is a function of the human being and is meant to serve the human life, its images humanized. I still see the connection between man and soul the other way around, as in the main Platonic tradition where man is a function of psyche and his job is to serve it. The therapist of psyche, which in root means "soul-servant," translates human events into the language of the psyche, rather than the psyche into the language of humanism.

[margin: human in service of psyche, rather than psyche in service of human]

At the front of therapy's secular humanism flies the banner of feeling. Where the Church and then psychoanalysis did not quite drive out the devils, 'personal relatedness in a human context' will finally do the job. The anima will become socially presentable, adapted. But if, as Jung says, "the Gods have become diseases,"[a] then curing the soul of its unrelated, inhuman images may also cure it of its Gods. The confusion of anima with feeling, and the attempt to humanize by feeling, is thus not psychotherapy at all. Rather it is part of contemporary secularism's sickness of soul, or psychopathology. We have yet to discover which archetypal person has captured consciousness through the sentimental appeal of humanism and feeling. At least we know it is not Eros, who prefers the dark and silence to 'relatedness,' 'communicating,' and 'sharing.' Yet some archetypal power does influence therapy by interpreting the psychic movement of our images and their animal–daimonic forms into social relations and personal connections and by raising such guilt over 'unrelatedness.' I suspect Hera, especially in her 'young-married' form of Hebe.

49

(a) The *anima* is the archetype of the feminine and plays a very important role in a man's unconscious.   CW 5, §406n142

> . . . the feminine figure of the anima . . . requires a different evalua-
> tion and position. . . . [A] personalistic interpretation always re-
> duces her to the personal mother or some other female person. The
> real meaning of the figure naturally gets lost in the process. . . .
> [S]he is more or less immortal, because outside time.
>   . . . [T]he archetypes . . . are unconsciously projected upon more
> or less suitable human personalities.   CW 9, i, §§356–57

> When projected, the anima always has a feminine form with def-
> inite characteristics. This empirical finding does not mean that the
> archetype is constituted like that *in itself*.   CW 9, i, §142

> . . . a man's consciousness projects all perceptions coming from the
> feminine personification of the unconscious onto an anima figure,
> i.e., a real woman. . . .   CW 10, §714

(b) We encounter the anima historically above all in the divine syzygies, the male-female pairs of deities. These reach down . . . into
. . . classical Chinese philosophy, where the cosmogonic pair of
concepts are designated *yang* (masculine) and *yin* (feminine).
   CW 9, i, §120

> In Eastern symbolism the square . . . has the character of the *yoni*:
> femininity. A man's unconscious is likewise feminine and is person-
> ified by the anima.   CW 12, §192

> . . . the heavenly bride . . . is a typical anima projection. . . .
> Spitteler also likens the "Lady Soul" to a tiger. (In China, the tiger
> is a symbol of *yin*.)   CW 13, §460 (and n14)

4. Anima and The Feminine

We NOW come to two definitions which put in question anima as image of man's contrasexual genetic structure and experience. Jung calls anima "the archetype of the feminine"[a] and "the archetype of life." He further draws analogies between anima and yin[b] and the Chinese *p'o* soul; between anima and the Indian

(a) The spiritual man was seduced into putting on the body, and was bound to it by "Pandora, whom the Hebrews call Eve." She played the part, therefore, of the anima . . . just as Shakti or Maya entangles man's consciousness with the world.　　　CW 13, §126

. . . the deceptive Shakti, must return to the watery realm if the work is to reach its goal. She should no longer dance before the adept with alluring gestures, but must become what she was from the beginning: a part of his wholeness. (The anima is thereby forced into the inner world. . . .)　　　CW 13, §223 (and n15)

He will learn to know his soul, that is, his anima and Shakti who conjures up a delusory world for him.　　　CW 14, §673

What, then, is this projection-making factor? The East calls it the "Spinning Woman" – Maya, who creates illusion by her dancing. (I have defined the anima as a personification of the unconscious.)　　　CW 9, ii, §20 (and n1)

. . . she is the great illusionist, the seductress, who draws him into life with her Maya. . . .
　　　. . . I have suggested . . . the term "anima". . . .
　　　　　　　　　　　　　　　　CW 9, ii, §§24–25

(b) As a psychopomp she [Sophia] leads the way to God and assures immortality.　　　CW 11, §613

Looked at theologically, my concept of the anima . . . is pure Gnosticism. . . .　　　CW 11, §460

The emotional state of Sophia sunk in unconsciousness . . . , her formlessness, and the possibility of her getting lost in the darkness characterize very clearly the anima of a man who identifies himself absolutely with his reason and his spirituality.　　　CW 13, §454 ideas of Maya and Shakti;[a] and he relates anima to the Gnostic Sophia (wisdom) (see index to CW 11 and CW 14, but especially CW 11, §613 where the description of Sophia as psychopomp has rich 'anima characteristics,' and CW 11, §460, where anima is called "pure Gnosticism").[b]

At this level we can hardly attribute anima to the male sex only. The "feminine" and "life" as well as the Chinese, Indian, and Gnostic analogies to anima are relevant to men and women equally. We are now at an archetypal level of anima, the "feminine archetypal image" (CW 9, ii, §41n5), and an archetype as such cannot be attributed to or located within the psyche of either sex. We may take this yet one step further, for we cannot be sure that the archetypes are only psychic, belonging only to the realm of psyche, unless we extend psyche first beyond sexual differences, then beyond the human person and psychodynamics (compensation), and beyond psychology too. Jung already made this extension in his notion of the archetype as psychoid, stating that "the archetypes,

(a) ... the archetypes are not found exclusively in the psychic sphere. ...   CW 8, §964

Although there is no form of existence that is not mediated to us psychically ... it would hardly do to say that everything is merely psychic. We must apply this argument logically to the archetypes as well.   CW 8, §420

(b) There are certain types of women who seem to be made by nature to attract anima projections; indeed one could almost speak of a definite "anima type." The so-called "sphinx-like" character is an indispensable part of their equipment, also an equivocalness, an intriguing elusiveness ... an indefiniteness that seems full of promises, like the speaking silence of a Mona Lisa.   CW 17, §339

I have seen Mrs. X. and I assure you she is quite an eyeful and beyond! ... If ever there was an anima it is she. ...
                              21 September 1951, Letter to Father Victor White

(c) The "maiden" corresponds to the anima of the man. ... But as long as a woman is content to be a *femme à homme*, she has no feminine individuality. She is empty and merely glitters – a welcome vessel for masculine projections.   CW 9, i, §355

If a mother-complex in a woman does not produce an overdeveloped Eros, it leads to identification with the mother and to paralysis of the daughter's feminine initiative. ... These bloodless maidens. ... are so empty that a man is free to impute to them anything he fancies. In addition, they are so unconscious that the unconscious puts out countless invisible feelers, veritable octopus-tentacles, that suck up all masculine projections; and this pleases men enormously.   CW 9, i, §169

therefore have a nature that *cannot with certainty be designated as psychic*" (CW 8, §439).[a] An adequate notion of anima thus requires that one look beyond men and beyond man, and even beyond psyche. But a metaphysics or metapsychics of the anima is not our direction here. Rather, it is to realize that <u>anima, as archetype, is too wide to be contained by the notion of contrasexuality (chapter one)</u>. <u>Anima, released from this containing definition, bears upon the psyche of women too.</u>

According to the first notion (contrasexuality), there is no anima in women. "The anima, being of feminine gender, is exclusively a figure that compensates the masculine consciousness" (CW 7, §328). "[T]he same figure is not to be found in the imagery of a woman's unconscious" (CW 11, §48). In accordance with the yoke of opposites women have the animus instead.

But what of "anima women," those women who play the anima for men and are called in analytical psychology "anima types."[b] Jung says that such women can best play this anima part by being empty themselves.[c] They therefore catch the projections of men, mirroring and mimicking them, so that a man's inner woman is lived out by an anima type.

(a) The anima is indeed the archetype of life itself. . . .   CW 14, §646

. . . the anima, who expresses *life* . . .   CW 14, §313

. . . the anima is the *archetype of life itself.*   CW 9, i, §66

(b) . . . now a good fairy, now a witch; now a saint, now a whore. . . .
the anima also has "occult" connections with "mysteries". . . . [S]he
is more or less immortal, because outside time. . . . [T]he anima . . .
belongs to a different order of things.   CW 9, i, §356

The anima also has affinities with animals, which symbolize her
characteristics. Thus she can appear as a snake or a tiger or a bird.
   CW 9, i, §358

For, besides the romantic idealizations of anima, she can also be tawdry, trite, trivial, barren, and cheap. And men can spend hours, years, in nothingness with a silly 'anima-type,' fluff and prattle. Seven years Ulysses passed in Calypso's cavernous emptiness. Why? What for? Hedonism? Incarnation into the flesh? Or is it to rescue and transform the woman, like Orpheus seeking to bring Eurydice to the upper light? Rather, this 'anima-type' presents us with an archetypal condition of soul that is drowsily nymphic, neither asleep nor awake, neither self-sustainingly virginal nor faithfully conjoined, lost and empty, a tabula rasa. Perhaps Eurydice wants to remain marginal, a shade insubstantial, and therefore the long years of escapes to dark bars and motel contraceptions, the mute waste in a limbo without light and without depth are a style of anima fascinations in which the absence of significance is precisely the significance. Anima, as archetype of life,[a] can be utterly devoid of meaning. Hence, she constellates the search for the wise old Man, archetype of meaning.

Here again I believe we have an instance of our psychic premises being determined by an archetypal figure so that we see that which is already given in the premise. We call these women anima types and we connect them with the ancient figure of the hetaera; yet because of theory (no anima in women), we assume that the anima archetype can affect a woman's life only through men and their fatuous projections.

Let us look at this more closely. The roles which Jung assigns to the anima[b] – relation with the mysteries, with the archaic past, enactment of the good fairy, witch, whore, saint, and animal associations with bird, tiger, and serpent (to mention only those he there mentions) – all appear frequently and validly in the psychology of women. Anima phenomenology is not restricted to the male sex. Women have little girls in their dreams, and whores; they too are lured by mysterious and unknown women. The Saint, Sappho, and Sleeping Beauty are part of their inscapes too. And as the images are not restricted to men only, so anima emotion cannot be confined only to the male sex. Women too bear an expectancy, an interiority that is opposed to their outer persona actions. They too lose touch and may be drawn away to meditate their fate, their death, their immortality. They too sense soul and suffer its mystery

(a) ... I have reserved the term "animus" strictly for women. . . .
Feminine psychology exhibits an element that is the counterpart of
a man's anima.   CW 13, §60

... a man in trying to attain his ideal of manhood represses all
feminine traits – which are really part of him, just as masculine
traits are part of a woman's psychology. . . . If we carefully examine the uncontrolled emotions of a man . . . we soon arrive at a
feminine figure which I call . . . the anima. On the same ground the
ancients conceived of a feminine soul, a "psyche" or "anima". . . .
                                                         CW 10, §79

and confusion. We say of a woman "she has soul," and we mean much the same as when we say this of a man.

Women are as salty in their weeping and resentments, as bitchy in their gossip, as abysmal in their dour brooding as men. The intensifications, exaggerations, and mythologizings that belong to the description of anima do appear in women and may not be ascribed to her unconscious feminine personality, the woman within, or attributed to a minority of female genes. Here the anima, archetype of life and archetype of the feminine, influences the psychic process regardless of sex, and we are freed from the masculine–feminine fantasy of anima, from the endless oscillations of compensation, and also from the epistemological deceit of explanations through "projection."

Why do we call the same behavior in one sex "anima" and in the other "naturally feminine" or "shadow"? What effect does this have on the psychological differences between the sexes, if the same image in a man and a woman is in his case ennobled as a soul-image (anima) while in hers it is part of the realm of shadow? By depriving by definition women of anima – "Woman has no anima, no soul, but she has an *animus*" (CW 17, §338)[a] – is not analytical psychology willy-nilly continuing a very ancient tradition of denying woman soul and casting the images of this soul into shadow? This is to doubt neither the reality of her shadow nor the pressing spiritual question in woman that is figured by animus.

But I do doubt that woman's psychological development means animus development, for this is an erosion of the categories of psyche and spirit. Animus refers to spirit, to logos, word, idea, intellect, principle, abstraction, meaning, *ratio*, *nous*. The discrimination of spirit is not at all of the same order as the cultivation of soul. If the first is active mind in its broadest sense, the second is the realm of the imaginal, equally embracing, but very different.

The assumption has been that because women are of the feminine gender they have soul – or rather are soul. As long as soul and femininity are an identity, then of course the soul problem of women is taken care of, again by definition, and by biology. (Freud, in his lecture on femininity, found himself in the same dilemma which he casts onto women as theirs: "You too will have pondered over this question [the nature of femininity] in so far as you are men; from the women among you that is not to be expect-

ed, for you are the riddle yourselves.")[22] But psyche, the sense of soul, is not given to woman just because she is born female. She is no more blessed with a congenitally saved soul than man who must pass his life in worry over its fate. She is no more exonerated from the tasks of anima cultivation than man; for her to neglect soul for the sake of spirit is no less psychologically reprehensible than it is in man who is ever being told by analytical psychology that he must sacrifice intellect, persona, and extraversion for the sake of soul, feeling, inwardness, i.e., anima.

[margin handwritten note: woman must cultivate soul, anima, just as man must]

The immense difficulty which some women have with imagination and the torment some go through in regard to a sense of inner emptiness both point to soul as area of their need. No less than men, women need fantasy, mythologizings in which they can read themselves and discover fate. To find a sense of worth, confidence as a person, or "psychological faith" as Grinnell[23] has called it, is as much a need of woman as of man. The hokey substitutes for soul, the anima sentimentalities and anima inflations, are found equally in both sexes; women's attempts at depth, inwardness, sensitivity, and wisdom are as prey to pseudo-soul as those of men. In women perhaps pseudo-soul is even more evident, for in the absence of anima, animus fills the gap, a transvestite travesty.

Animus is given with the civilization, and its psychic representation which we foreshorten into the notion of ego is, as Neumann[24] pointed out, masculine in women too. Ego's archetype is the Hero, and so its underside in women too will show the soulful qualities of anima. The neglected area is not animus but anima.

An animus development with which anima does not keep pace will lead a woman away from psychological understanding. This occurs by drying her fantasy, narrowing her range of mood and involvement with life, turning her into at best a spiritual paragon and a psychological dunce, her wisdom, her concern, her counsel all being developed opinion, detached, rather than soul reflection in the midst of her attachments – and this we see even where the preferred field of animus development be psychology itself. The domain of psychology does not guarantee that its inhabitants are particularly psychological. The shingle over the door, "psychologist," unfortunately attests to nothing about the soul of the practitioner. And if the practitioner be a woman, then the epithet "psychologist" even more certainly has nothing to do with soul,

61

(a)   But as long as a woman is content to be a *femme à homme*, she has no feminine individuality. She is empty and merely glitters – a welcome vessel for masculine projections.   CW 9, i, §355

(b)   . . . the Kore often appears in woman as an *unknown young girl*, not infrequently as Gretchen or the unmarried mother. . . . [or] the *dancer*, . . . the *corybant*, *maenad*, or *nymph*.

                                                        CW 9, i, §311

since the (animus) developmental process which led to the title has been by definition one of spirit, not of soul. To state this implies nothing against the development of logos or against respect for ideas in women, but as spirit is not soul, so animus is not anima, and neither can be neglected nor substituted for the other. The syzygy means both.

The power of our theoretical notions cannot be overestimated. By our denying woman anima and giving her animus instead, an entire archetypal pattern has been determined for women's psychology. The *per definitionem* absence of anima in women is a deprivation of a cosmic principle with no less consequence in the practice of analytical psychology than has been the theory of penis deprivation in the practice of psychoanalysis.

While raising this doubt about the animus, I would as well raise a hope that the typically anima constellations in a woman's psyche be treated as such, and no longer as shadow simply because these manifestations are feminine. This in turn would lead to a more precisely refined notion of shadow, perhaps keeping it reserved for the *morally* repressed. Whenever it comes to a choice between saving the theory and saving the phenomena, the history of thought shows that it profits more to side with the phenomena, even if for a while theory is dislocated and some things we had considered clear fall back into a new obscurity.

Returning now to the emptiness of the anima-type woman, we may remember that hitherto her relationship to the anima archetype has had by definition to come through a man. But now we may no longer regard her psychology in this way. The emptiness is no mere void for catching a projection from the opposite sex. Nor may we account for this emptiness through the notions of an unconscious shadow or an undeveloped animus. To derive it from a father-complex again puts the origin onto man, leaving the woman only a daughter, only an object created by projection, an Eve born out of Adam's sleep, without independent soul, fate, and individuality.[a]

Rather this emptiness would be considered an authentic archetypal manifestation of the anima in one of her classical forms, maiden, nymph, Kore, which Jung so well describes,[b] and where he also states that "she often appears in woman." Even should we

(a) Melusina comes into the same category as the nymphs and sirens who dwell in the "Nymphidida," the watery realm.... [T]he birthplace of Melusina is the womb of the mysteries, obviously what we today would call the unconscious.... Melusina is clearly an anima figure. CW 13, §180

... Melusina, the water-nixie, ... [can] change herself into human form. Dorn thinks of this as a "vision appearing in the mind" and not as a projection on a real woman....

... The anima belongs to those borderline phenomena which chiefly occur in special psychic situations.... One is confronted with a hopeless and impenetrable darkness, an abysmal void that is now suddenly filled with an alluring vision, the palpably real presence of a strange yet helpful being....

This peculiarity of the anima is found ... in the Melusina legend.... CW 13, §§215–17

Mythologically, nymphs, dryads, etc. are nature- and tree-numina, but psychologically they are anima projections....

CW 14, §70

(b) When projected, the anima always has a feminine form with definite characteristics. This empirical finding does not mean that the archetype is constituted like that *in itself*. CW 9, i, §142

relate this maiden to the daughter, it may remain within the anima constellation. There is no need to search outside for origins in a father.

We all know that fathers create daughters; but daughters create fathers too. The enactment of the maiden-daughter in all her receptive charm, shy availability, and masochistic wiliness draws down a fathering spirit. But its appearance and her victimization are her creation. Even the idea that she is all a result of the father (or the absent or bad father) is part of the father-fantasy of the anima archetype. And so, she must be 'so attached' to father because anima is reflection of an attachment. She creates the figurative father and the belief in its responsibility which serves to confirm the archetypal metaphor of Daughter that owes its source, not to the father, but to the anima inherent in a woman's psyche, too.

Moreover, the muse, to whom the nymph has a special connection and toward whom her consciousness is intending, if we follow W.F. Otto,[25] belongs also authentically to the potential of women's psychology in its own right and is not only in reflection to men. It is not *man's* anima, and so it is not a man's inner life that the nymph, hetaera, or muse is reflecting but anima as archetype, which by other names is psyche or soul.[a]

At this level of distinction Jung himself raises a doubt whether we can truly speak of the anima per se as feminine. He suggests that we may have to confine the archetype's femininity to its projected form.[b] Paradoxically, the very archetype of the feminine may not itself be feminine. (Cf. 8 June 1959, Letter to Traugott Egloff: "The androgyny of the anima may appear in the anima herself. . . .") One could raise a similar doubt about the "femininity" of life of which anima is the archetype.

(a)   . . . [in] classical Chinese philosophy . . . the anima (*p'o* or *kuei*) is regarded as the feminine and chthonic part of the soul.

CW 9,i, §119

. . . I used the term "anima" in a way quite analogous to the Chinese definition of *p'o*. . . . [T]he affective character of a man has feminine traits. From this psychological fact derives the Chinese doctrine of the *p'o* soul as well as my own concept of the anima.

CW 13, §58

"Anima," called *p'o*, and written with the characters for "white" and "demon," that is, "white ghost," belongs to the lower, earth-bound, bodily soul, the *yin* principle, and is therefore feminine.

CW 13, §57

(b)   . . . the anima is the *archetype of life itself.*   CW 9,i, §66

Being that has soul is living being. Soul is the living thing in man, that which lives of itself and causes life. . . . With her cunning play of illusions the soul lures into life the inertness of matter that does not want to live. She makes us believe incredible things, that life may be lived. She is full of snares and traps, in order that man should fall, should reach the earth, entangle himself there, and stay caught. . . .   CW 9,i, §56

The contentless asexual description of the anima archetype as "life," analogous with Maya, Shakti, Sophia, and the *p'o* soul,[a] points to a specific kind of life, life which projects out of itself consciousness. In other words, the life which Jung[b] attributes to the anima archetype is *psychic life*: "The anima. . . . is a 'factor' in the proper sense of the word. Man cannot make it; on the contrary, it is always the *a priori* element in his moods, reactions, impulses, and whatever else is spontaneous in psychic life. It is something that lives of itself, that makes us live; it is a life behind consciousness that cannot be completely integrated with it, but from which, on the contrary, consciousness arises" (CW 9, i, §57).

(a) In the case of an anima-possession, for instance, the patient will want to change himself into a woman through self-castration, or he is afraid that something of the sort will be done to him by force. The best-known example of this is Schreber's *Memoirs of My Nervous Illness*. Patients often discover a whole anima mythology with numerous archaic motifs.   CW 9, i, §82

(b) The psoriasis of the anima figure is due to certain contents which the anima has within her, as though in the blood, and which sweat out on the surface. This is also indicated by the snakelike patterns of the psoriasis. It is a kind of painting that appears on the skin. Very often this points to the need to portray certain contents or states graphically, and in colour.... This "art" activity.... these works of the anima are products of the feminine mind in a man. The feminine mind is pictorial and symbolic and comes close to what the ancients called Sophia.

22 March 1935, Letter to Dr. S.

To consider anima as the life behind consciousness from which consciousness arises deepens our understanding of her strange expressions in images, emotions, and symptoms. She projects herself into consciousness through expression; expression is her art, whether in the extraordinary artfulness of symptom formation and clinical 'picture'[a] or the artifices of anima bewitchments. And the wisdom that Sophia imparts is seeing sophically into these expressions, seeing the art in the symptom.[b]

Anima here is not a projection but is the projector. And our consciousness is the result of her prior psychic life. Anima thus becomes the primordial carrier of psyche, or the archetype of psyche itself.

(a) Anima means soul. . . . [T]he soul is the magic breath of life (hence the term "anima"). . . . CW 9, i, §55

But I should be carrying brevity too far if I described the anima merely as a primordial image of woman consisting of irrational feelings, and the animus merely as a primordial image of man consisting of irrational views. Both figures present . . . elementary forms of that psychic phenomenon which from primitive times has been called "soul." They are also the cause of that deep human need to speak of souls or daemons at all. CW 10, §82

. . . the queen and the king are one, in the sense that body and soul or spirit and soul are one. . . . the queen corresponds to the soul (anima). . . . CW 14, §536 (cf. CW 10, §243; CW 13, §168n62)

The archaic souls, the *ba* and *ka* of the Egyptians, are complexes of this kind. At a still higher level, . . . this complex is invariably of the feminine gender – anima. . . . CW 7, §295

(b) Anima means soul and should designate something very wonderful and immortal. Yet this was not always so. We should not forget that this kind of soul is a dogmatic conception whose purpose it is to pin down and capture something uncannily alive and active. CW 9, i, §55

Here I would like to guard against a misunderstanding. The concept of "soul" which I am now using can be compared more with the primitive idea of the soul . . . than with the Christian idea of it, which is an attempt to make a philosophical construct. . . . My conception of the soul has absolutely nothing to do with this. . . . CW 10, §84 (cf. CW 7, §§302, 371)

5. Anima and Psyche

W E   A R E led to another consideration: the relation of anima to psyche itself. In many places[a] Jung uses anima and soul interchangeably. Nevertheless, he applies his main effort to the difficult task of keeping distinct the three terms – anima, soul, psyche. From one side he differentiates anima from soul, saying, "I have suggested instead the term 'anima,' as indicating something specific, for which the expression 'soul' is too general and too vague" (CW 9, ii, §25). He wants to make sure that his concept, 'anima,' is not confused with the traditional ideas of soul in religion and philosophy.[b] From another side he also wants to define anima so that it does not refer to psyche, of which it is only one archetype. Neither soul nor anima can be identified with the "totality of the psychic functions" (CW 6, §420). For this totality the term "self" is

71

(a) [In the German text the word *Anima* is used only twice....
Everywhere else the word used is *Seele* (soul). In this translation
anima is substituted for "soul" when it refers specifically to the
feminine component in a man.... "Soul" is retained only when it
refers to the psychic factor common to both sexes. The distinction
is not always easy to make....]   CW 6, §803n80

[... there is no consistent equivalent of *Seele* in English.... in
the essay "Spirit and Life," ... "soul" would give entirely the
wrong meaning. It has therefore been translated ... either as "psyche" or as "mind".... [There is] an increasing tendency to re-
place the concept *Seele* by *Psyche*, until, in "The Real and the Sur-
real" (1933), *Psyche* alone occupies the field.]   CW 8, p. 300

[The translation of ... *Seele* presents almost insuperable difficulties ... because it combines the two words "psyche" and
"soul"....
    ... either *Psyche* or *Seele* – has been used with reference to the
totality of *all* psychic processes.... "Soul," on the other hand, ...
is more restricted in meaning and refers to a "function complex" or
partial personality.... It is often applied specifically to "anima"
and "animus"....]   CW 12, §9n2

generally reserved. (For more on these differentiations see the editors' and translator's notes.)[a]

In another context[26] I attempted to separate some of the threads in the nexus 'anima,' 'psyche,' 'soul.' I suggested there that the moods and behavior peculiar to what analytical psychology calls anima are best seen against the archetypal background of Psyche in Apuleius's tale and that, therefore, this anima behavior was precisely where to look for the emergence of psyche. My point there was to show *phenomenologically* that what starts out as mere anima moods and fantasies becomes psychological ambiguity, that is, receptivity, containment and imagination, so that the way to psychological understanding is through anima. My point here is to show *conceptually* that the process of anima becoming psyche can be deduced from Jung's notion of anima itself. In fact, I think a case can be made for another definition of anima: *archetype of psyche*. Although this definition does not directly appear in Jung, it can be derived from Jung in the following ways:

(a) ... Prakrti dancing before Purusha in order to remind him of "dis-criminating knowledge," does not belong to the mother archetype but to the archetype of the anima. ...   CW 9, i, §158

Nor is she [the anima] a substitute figure for the mother.
                                                    CW 9, ii, §26

We may ... assume that the transferring of the water of life to the sister really means that the mother has been replaced by the anima.
                                                    CW 12, §92

... the anima appears equally as maiden and mother, which is why a personalistic interpretation always reduces her to the per-sonal mother or some other female person. The real meaning of the figure naturally gets lost in the process. ...   CW 9, i, §356

a) Jung associates a host of feminine forms with anima; but one in particular he generally keeps outside its confines. This is the mother. "The most striking feature about the anima-type is that the maternal element is lacking."[a] The anima makes possible a "purely human relationship" independent of the maternal element of procreation[27] (CW 10, §76). Anima thus represents the movement into adulthood and the "growth away from nature" (ibid.).

In alchemy the growth away from nature is spoken of as the *opus contra naturam*, a key concept for the *psychological*, in distinction to the *naturalistic*, understanding of psychic events. The movement from mother to anima represents this shift in perspective from naturalistic to psychological understanding. In alchemy the relationship corresponding with the psychological perspective was exemplified in the adept's relationship with an anima-*soror*. The psychological approach essential to alchemy required anima, so that she becomes the archetypal premise of psychological work.

(a) ... two empirically very common archetypes, namely the anima and the Wise Old Man, flow together in the symbolic phenomenology of Mercurius. CW 12, §218

... Mercurius is the *anima mundi*. CW 9, ii, §212

Soul, from Old German *saiwalô*, may be cognate with αἰόλος, 'quick-moving, changeful of hue, shifting.' It also has the meaning of 'wily' or 'shifty'; hence an air of probability attaches to the alchemical definition of *anima* as Mercurius. CW 9, i, §391n5

Mercurius is often designated as *anima*....
... Very much more material is the definition of Mercurius as a "life-giving power like a glue, holding the world together and standing in the middle between body and spirit." This concept corresponds to ... Mercurius as the *anima media natura*. From here it is but a step to the identification of Mercurius with the *anima mundi*.... CW 13, §§262–63

As the *anima mundi*, Mercurius can in fact be compared with the Gnostic ... (virgin of light) and with the Christian Virgin Mary.... CW 12, §506

... outwardly Mercurius corresponds to quicksilver but inwardly he is ... an *anima mundi*.... CW 14, §699

(b) I have defined the anima as a personification of the unconscious. CW 9, ii, §20n1

... the unconscious is often personified by the anima.... CW 11, §107

... the anima ... represents the collective unconscious. CW 14, §128

b) In a series of passages Jung demonstrates the identity of anima and Mercurius.[a] Mercurius receives various anima and soul names; and, as Mercurius is called (CW 13, §299) "the archetype of the unconscious," so the anima is the archetype who "personifies the collective unconscious" (CW 10, §714).[b]

Mercurius and anima have similarly shifty, flighty, iridescent, hard-to-catch, hard-to-fathom natures, a quality imaged by quicksilver in Mercurius and by the anima as elf and Melusine, and by the shimmering wings of *psyché*. Their similarity does not make them one in all respects, but it does help substantiate the idea that the special significance of anima is psychic, since Mercurius is the representation par excellence of psychic nature. (I believe their identity is more pronounced when soul and spirit have not been discriminated; then anima is exaggeratedly mercurial, less the container than seductively elusive – all over the place – and then the spirit is predominately moist, vaporous, and in a soulful flux of uncertainties. It is in this condition when soul and spirit are confounded that the spirit is garbed in white, her color [the *albedo, anima candida*], and soul appears dressed by his blue or his red. Some of the 'puella' phenomena in young women express this mixture of spirit and soul: an unfixed mercurial spirit that acts as fascinating spark in a soul innocent of what it contains.)

(a) ... the queen and the king are one, in the sense that body and soul or spirit and soul are one.... the queen corresponds to the soul (anima) and the king to spirit. ... the secret of the work was sometimes called the "Reginae Mysteria." CW 14, §536

... our picture represents the union of the spirit with material reality.... [T]he spirit of the gold, [is] only the right half of the king.... The queen is a sulphur, ... a chthonic spirit.... [T]he self or imago Dei ... is here united with its chthonic counterpart. ... [T]his is personified in the psychological anima figure.... [T]he alchemical queen ... corresponds to the psychological anima. CW 14, §736

(b) [For Richard White] ... The human soul is "androgynous," "because a girl has a masculine and a man a feminine soul." ... [He] adds ... the soul is also called an "old woman"....

... [H]e writes that the soul is an idea "of such great power that she creates the forms and things themselves," also "she has within herself the 'selfness' of all mankind." She transcends all individual differences.... It should be noted that he describes this soul quite differently from the way it would be described by a biological or personalistic psychology today.... CW 14, §§92–93

c) But the basic alchemical cluster of ideas associated with anima is that of Luna and Regina and their many other names for the one component of the arcane pair. This component, which, following Jung,[a] we abbreviate here by Regina, is regarded alchemically in one conjunction to be the counterpart of body, while in another conjunction she becomes the counterpart of spirit. Jung lets Regina stand equally for the feminine, for eros, for soul, the unconscious, the anima, and for the psyche. That is to say, in these alchemical syzygies Regina means psyche itself when psyche is imagined to be different from body or different from spirit.

We should note here that Jung employs the term *psyche* in two senses. In the narrower and traditional usage, psyche is the soul component of the conjunction. It is in this sense that psyche is phenomenologically and terminologically indistinguishable from anima. In the broader usage, and one rather specific to Jung, psyche means more than a component and therefore cannot be equated with the anima archetype. Psyche in this sense means all the processes depicted in alchemy, including body, spirit, sun and moon, mercurius, etc. They are each psychological; they are all taking place in the psyche. Anima would only be one of these factors.

This sort of extended notion of soul appears in alchemy, e.g., the soul described by Richard White[b] which, Jung points out, differs extremely from the idea of psyche in "biological and personalistic psychology." This soul is at once the personified anima figured in a female form and the reflective psychological principle. As Jung notes, she joins in one the distinction between the wider notion of soul (*anima mundi*) and the narrower one (*anima vagula*). This distinction between soul and *the* soul or *my* soul did not bother the alchemists, and it was a distinction upon which Neoplatonism refused to insist, for Plotinus was able to discuss psychology on both levels at once: what takes place in psyche of course takes place in man's soul. Archetypal psychology is of course reflected within an individual psyche. Jung sometimes concurs, saying for instance (CW 16, §469), "it often seems advisable to speak less of *my* anima or *my* animus and more of *the* anima and *the* animus. As archetypes, these figures are semi-collective and impersonal quantities. . . ." He also regrets (CW 11, §759) that: "Man himself has ceased to be the microcosm and eidolon of the cosmos, and his 'anima' is no longer the consubstantial *scintilla*, or

(a) ... when anima forfeits the daemonic power of an autonomous complex ... she is depotentiated. ... no longer is the soul to be called "Mistress," but a psychological function of an intuitive nature, akin to what the primitives mean when they say, "He has gone into the forest to talk with the spirits" or "My snake spoke with me". ...   CW 7, §374

(b) The soul functions ... in the body, but has the greater part of its function ... outside the body. ...   CW 12, §396

spark of the *Anima Mundi,* the World Soul." Because we take the anima personalistically, or she dupes the ego this way, we lose the wider significance of anima. This loss of soul goes on even while we are most engaged in the attempt to gain it: "developing *my* anima" through relatedness, creativity, and individuation.

Unless we understand the "within" in a radically new way – or classically old way – we go on perpetuating the division between my anima and world soul (objective psyche). The more we concentrate her inside and literalize interiority within my person, the more we lose the sense of soul as a psychic reality interiorly within all things. Anima within is not merely within my breast; introjection and internalization do not mean making my head or my skin the vessel inside of which all psychic processes take place. The "within" refers to that attitude given by the anima which perceives psychic life within natural life. Natural life itself becomes the vessel the moment we recognize its having an interior significance, the moment we see that it too bears and carries psyche. Anima makes vessels everywhere, anywhere, by going within.[a]

The means of doing this is fantasy. Phenomena come alive and carry soul through our imaginative fantasies about them. When we have no fantasy about the world, then it is objective, dead; even the fantasy of pollution helps bring the world back to life as having significance for soul. Fantasy is not merely an interior process going on in my head. It is a way of being in the world and giving back soul to the world.

The attempt to take back soul from life outside deprives the outside of its "within," stuffing the person with subjective soulfulness and leaving the world a slagheap from which all projections, personifications, and psyche have been extracted. For this reason, the more we work at our own personalities and subjectivities in the name of the anima, the less we are truly soul-making and the more we are continuing in the illusion that anima is in us rather than we in it. Psyche is the wider notion than man, and man functions by virtue of psyche and is dependent upon it rather than the other way round: "man ... is ... in *the* psyche (not in *his* psyche)" (14 May 1950, Letter to Joseph Goldbrunner). "The greater part of the soul is outside the body," says Jung, quoting the alchemist Sendivogius (12 July 1951, Letter to Karl Kerényi).[b] Because the anima notion always implicates the world-soul, or soul of and in the world, a de-

(a) Although neither anima nor animus can be constellated without the intervention of the conscious personality, this does not mean that the resultant situation is nothing but a personal relationship... [W]e are dealing with an archetype which is anything but personal. CW 16, §469

velopment of anima-consciousness never takes place merely through the development of individual subjectivity.

'My' anima expresses the *personalistic fallacy*. Even though anima experiences bring with them a numinosity of person, the feeling of a unique inwardness and sense of importance (exaggerations and mythologizations of mood, insight, or fantasy), to take these experiences literally, as literally personal, puts anima inside '*me*.' The heightened subjectivity of anima events "is anything but personal" because it is archetypal.[a] The anima is the archetype behind these personalisms, and therefore the experiences are archetypally personal, making us feel both archetypal and personal at one and the same instant. But to take the archetypal literally as personal is a personalistic fallacy. So, when under the domination of anima our soulfulness makes us feel most uniquely 'me,' special, different, called – this is precisely the moment when, as Jung goes on to say in the same passage, "we are in fact most estranged from ourselves and most like the average type of *Homo sapiens*."

Returning now to the dilemma arising from the two senses of anima – the narrower meaning of one component in the coniunctio and the wider meaning of the region in which the entire process takes place – we may understand it as follows: anima may be only one ingredient in the alchemy of psychic processes. But because of her conjunctive role (*anima mercurius*), she is that factor through which it all occurs as psychic; she is the means by which (anima as copula and ligament) and in which (anima as vessel) the entire process takes place. Because of her these events become personally experienced as mine, going on in my soul. It is by virtue of the anima ingredient that events which are impersonal and only natural reactions or only spiritual ideas become psychic experiences.

Thus we find the idea in Jung that, the more realized the anima (as one archetypal factor in the psyche), the more "psychic existence becomes reality" (CW 16, §438). The reality of psyche as an all-too-convincing experience begins in the subjectivized moods and follies of the highly personalized anima. Nowhere do we more stubbornly encounter the reality of soul – in itself such a dim and wispy idea – than in the crosspatch nastiness of bad tempers, the insights that slip away, the sensitive vanities that will not be mollified. Within these commonplace disturbances, as Jung points out

(a) . . . the anima [can] continually thwart[s] the good intentions of the conscious mind, by contriving a private life that stands in sorry contrast to the dazzling persona. . . .

. . . [T]he "nothing but fantasy" attitude will never persuade me to regard my anima manifestations as anything more than fatuous weakness. If, however, I take the line that the world is outside *and* inside, . . . I must logically accept the upsets and annoyances that come to me from inside as symptoms of faulty adaptation to the conditions of that inner world.   CW 7, §§318–19

(b) . . . the *reflective instinct*. . . . *Reflexio* means 'bending back' . . . the fact that the reflex which carries the stimulus over into its instinctive discharge is interfered with by psychization. . . . *Reflexio* is a turning inwards, with the result that . . . there ensues a succession of derivative contents or states which may be termed reflection or deliberation.

Through the reflective instinct, the stimulus is more or less wholly transformed into a psychic content, that is, it becomes an experience. . . .   CW 8, §§241–43

(c) Luna . . . is the counterpart of Sol, cold, moist, feebly shining or dark, feminine, corporeal, passive. Accordingly her most significant role is that of a partner in the coniunctio. . . . [S]he is a universal receptacle, of the sun in particular; . . . she "receives and pours out" the powers of heaven. . . . [S]ilver is yet another synonym or symbol for the arcanum "Luna."   CW 14, §154

(d) In the shape of the goddess the anima is manifestly projected, but in her proper (psychological) shape she is *introjected*; she is . . . the "anima within." She is the natural *sponsa*, . . . the companion whom the endogamous tendency vainly seeks to win in the form of mother and sister. She represents that longing which has always had to be sacrificed. . . . Layard therefore speaks very rightly of "internalization through sacrifice."   CW 16, §438

in a detailed example extending through a whole chapter, is an anima fantasy;[a] and psychic existence also becomes reality when we recognize the driving power and full import of fantasy itself. Anima refers to a "quintessence of fantasy-images" (CW 14, §736) and an "'air-coloured' quintessence" (ibid., §749) whose final effect in bringing home the reality of the psyche is a realization "that this fantasy is happening, and it is as real as you – as a psychic entity – are real," "just as if you were one of the fantasy figures" (ibid., §753). My conviction that psyche and its fantasies are as real as matter and nature, as real as spirit, depends on how convincing anima has made herself to me. Thus on her depends the psychological calling.

d) The relation of anima and psyche comes out in yet one more way: through Jung's idea of reflection. On the five instinctual drives (hunger, sexuality, activity, reflection, and creation) upon which he elaborates, his notion of reflection[b] – "bending back" and "turning inwards" away from the world and its stimuli in favor of psychic images and experiences – correlates most closely with his notion of anima. Anima as Luna,[c] passive, cool, breeding, brooding, inward, describes reflection in alchemical language. The archetype corresponding with the instinct of reflection would be the anima.

Primordial images of this bending back and away are presented by the retreating but fecund nymphs and the illusionary voices and ephemera (moonlight, mists, echoes, musings, fantasies) of which we have spoken above and which I have discussed in more detail in relation with the feminine figures associated with Pan.[28] The turning inwards from the object in favor of internal images correlates again with the endogamous introjection of the anima, or "'internalization through sacrifice'" (CW 16, §438),[d] necessary for psychic consciousness. Another image of reflection associated traditionally with anima is the mirror and the activity of mirroring.

When Jung discourses briefly upon the nature of "unconscious reflection" (CW 11, §237), he says: "Where judgments and flashes of insight are transmitted by unconscious activity, they are often attributed to an archetypal feminine figure, the anima or mother-beloved. It then seems as if the inspiration came from the mother or from the beloved, the 'femme inspiratrice'" (CW 11, §240). At another level he speaks in his Seminars of the same unconscious

(a) Through his imagination the timid man has made his eyes basilisk-
like, and he infects the mirror, the moon, and the stars.... Thus
man in turn will be poisoned by this mirror of the moon.... And
as the mirror is defiled by the woman, thus conversely the eyes ...
are being defiled by the moon, for the reason that at such times the
eyes of the timid imagining man are weak and dull....

CW 14, §215

mental activity as "the 'natural mind'" (CW 9, i, §167n5), where we do not think but are thought, and he holds this natural mind to be exclusively a feminine property.

The autonomy of the instinct to reflect, which Jung calls the natural mind, appears in a more baleful context as the lunar mind described by Paracelsus in his *De pestilitate*,[a] a text Jung expands upon when discussing the poisonous and paralyzing aspect of reflection. The "lunar anima" (CW 14, §225) is evidently responsible for what Paracelsus calls the "disheartened" and "timid imagining man" who poisons and is poisoned by the mirror of the moon, so that the very instrument of reflection is damaged by a basilisk eye. These conditions of despairing introspection and foreboding speculation show the dark side of the moon where the instinct to "bend back" and "turn inwards" literalizes into a timid retreat from the bold heart required for what Paracelsus elsewhere calls "true imagining."

But the key passages which relate anima to psyche via reflection are these: "The richness of the human psyche and its essential character are probably determined by this reflective instinct" (CW 8, §242). Thus psyche is mainly a result of the instinct of reflection, which in turn is intimately tied with the anima archetype. "Through reflection, 'life' and its 'soul' are abstracted from Nature and endowed with a separate existence" (CW 11, §235). The archetype of both life and soul as distinct from 'only Nature' (procreative, biological Mother Nature) is anima, so that she would be that archetype which both performs the abstraction through reflection and personifies the life and soul in a reflected form. Anima is nature now conscious of itself through reflection. Or, as Jung puts it (ibid., §235n9): "reflection is a spiritual act that runs counter to the natural process; an act whereby we stop, call something to mind, form a picture, and take up a relation to and come to terms with what we have seen. It should, therefore, be understood as an act of *becoming conscious*."

Far-reaching consequences emerge from these passages. They indicate nothing less than an altogether other vision for the archetypal base of consciousness. If "becoming conscious" has its roots

(a) The anima is . . . a natural archetype that satisfactorily sums up all the statements of the unconscious, of the primitive mind, of the history of language and religion. . . . [I]t is always the *a priori* element in his moods, reactions, impulses, and whatever else is spontaneous in psychic life. It is something that lives of itself, that makes us live; it is a life behind consciousness that cannot be completely integrated with it, but from which, on the contrary, consciousness arises.
CW 9, i, §57

in reflection and if this instinct refers to the anima archetype, then consciousness itself may more appropriately be conceived as based upon anima than upon ego.

We have already heard Jung suggest as much, saying about the anima, "it is a life behind consciousness . . . from which . . . consciousness arises" (CW 9, i, §57).ᵃ He elaborates upon this notion when discussing the primitive idea that "the name of an individual is his soul" (CW 8, §665), which "means nothing less than that ego-consciousness is recognized as being an expression of the soul." He says further (ibid., §668) that "the sense of the 'I' – the ego-consciousness – grows out of unconscious life." And the life he speaks of in these passages is "soul." Again (CW 14, §129), when he says "our consciousness issues from a dark body, the ego," "full of unfathomable obscurities," a "mirror in which the unconscious becomes aware of its own face," we are given a description approaching that of the anima. This kind of ego is reflective; it is a complex of opposites; and like the anima it is defined as a "personification of the unconscious itself." In yet another significant passage Jung contrasts ego and anima as bases of consciousness. When commenting upon a Chinese text, he notes that there "consciousness (that is, personal consciousness) comes from the anima" and says the East "sees consciousness as an effect of the anima" (CW 13, §62). Here the two archetypal bases are contrasted by means of the East–West fantasy.

The ego as base of consciousness has always been an anachronistic part of analytical psychology.[29] It is a historical truth that our Western tradition has identified ego with consciousness, an identification that found formulation especially in nineteenth-century psychology and psychiatry. But this part of Jung's thought does not sit well with either his notion of psychic reality or his therapeutic goals of psychic consciousness. What brings cure is an archetypal consciousness (mediated by the anima as we know from other passages), and this notion of consciousness is definitely not based upon ego:

> It is as though, at the climax of the illness, the destructive powers were converted into healing forces. This is brought about by the archetypes awaking to independent life and taking over the guidance of the psychic personality, thus supplanting the ego with its futile willing and

89

(a) Consciousness consists in the relation of a psychic content to the
ego. Anything not associated with the ego remains unconscious.

CW 14, §522n400 (cf. CW 14, §131n68)

(b) When, therefore, an alchemist conjured up the spirit of Saturn as
his familiar, this was an attempt to bring to consciousness a standpoint outside the ego, involving a relativization of the ego and its
contents.   CW 14, §504 (cf. CW 9, ii, §11)

. . . there are good grounds for the prejudice that the ego is the cen-
tre of the personality, and that the field of consciousness is the psyche *per se*. . . . [I]t is only since the end of the nineteenth century
that modern psychology . . . has discovered the foundations of
consciousness and proved empirically the existence of a psyche
outside consciousness. With this discovery the position of the ego,
till then absolute, became relativized. . . . It is part of the personality but not the whole of it.   CW 9, ii, §11

striving. . . . the psyche has awakened to spontaneous activity. . . . something that is not his ego and is therefore beyond the reach of his personal
will. He has regained access to the sources of psychic life, and this marks
the beginning of the cure. (CW 11, §534)

The entire movement of Jung's work is away from ego and
toward a widening of consciousness that strikes its roots in and reflects other psychic dominants – yet, even in late work, he uses
"the word 'consciousness' here as being equivalent to 'ego'" (CW
14, §131n68).ᵃ This equivalence necessitates a series of compensatory operations, e.g., sacrifice of intellect, development of fourth
function, development of anima, introversion, shifting consciousness to the second-half of life and its focus on death, all of which is
summed up as the "relativization of the ego,"ᵇ for the sake of
"psychic consciousness."[30] But precisely this latter is a consciousness structured by the anima archetype.

Here I depart from Onians's analysis of *anima* in Roman contexts and follow Jung and Bachelard. Onians says: "*anima* has
nothing to do with consciousness." Much of what we commonly
mean by consciousness today belongs to *animus*: "Consciousness
with all the variations of emotion and thought is a matter of *animus*. To contemplate some action is 'to have it in one's animus'; to
turn one's attention to something . . . is 'to turn the *animus*
towards it'; . . . to feel faint, to be on the way to losing consciousness, was . . . 'it goes ill with one's *animus*'." "*Anima* was generic"[31] and thus a far vaguer term, to do with airs of all sorts, located in the head. But following Jung, every archetype, by forming
a pattern of behavior and a cluster of imagery, informs consciousness and has a kind of consciousness. If consciousness is defined as
it is today, and as Onians regards it, that is, mainly as attention
and self-referent experience, it is more an ego-consciousness and as
we suggested above is more associated with animus than anima.
Onians's statement in regard to Rome, "*Anima* has nothing to do
with consciousness," is applicable to today's term "anima," only if
we modify his statement to mean: anima has nothing to do with a
certain style of consciousness, namely, ego-consciousness. Likewise, Bachelard gives anima the consciousness of images, reverie,
and depths (and much more) and assigns to animus "projects and
worries," or what we usually call (ego-) 'consciousness.' "Animus

is a bourgeois with regular habits" again refers to the continuity of the ego and its adaptation to 'reality.'³²

The "relativization of the ego," that work and that goal of the fantasy of individuation, is made possible, however, from the beginning if we shift our conception of the base of consciousness from ego to anima archetype, from I to soul. Then one realizes from the very beginning (a priori and by definition) that the ego and all its developmental fantasies were never, even at the start, the fundament of consciousness, because consciousness refers to a process more to do with images than will, with reflection rather than control, with reflective insight into, rather than manipulation of, 'objective reality.' We would no longer be equating consciousness with one phase of it, the developmental period of youth and its questing heroic mythology. Then, too, while educating consciousness even in youth, the aim of nourishing anima would be no less significant than that of strengthening ego.

Instead of regarding anima from the viewpoint of ego where she becomes a poisonous mood, an inspiring weakness, or a contra-sexual compensation, we might regard ego from soul's perspective where ego becomes an instrument for day-to-day coping, nothing more grandiose than a trusty janitor of the planetary houses, a servant of soul-making. This view at least gives ego a therapeutic role rather than forcing it into the anti-therapeutic position, a stubborn old king to be relativized. Then, too, we might relativize the myth of the Hero, or take it for what it has become today for our psyche – the myth of inflation – and not the secret key to the development of human consciousness. The Hero-myth tells the tale of conquest and destruction, the tale of psychology's "strong ego," its fire and sword, as well as the career of its civilization, but it tells little of the culture of its consciousness. Strange that we could still, in a psychology as subtle as Jung's, believe that this King-Hero, and his ego, is the equivalent of consciousness. Images of this psychological equivalence were projected from television screens straight and live from the heroic-ego's great contemporary epic in Vietnam. Is this consciousness?

Basing consciousness upon soul accords with the Neoplatonic tradition – which we still find in Blake – where what today is called ego-consciousness would be the consciousness of the Platonic cave, a consciousness buried in the least aware perspectives.

(a) . . . only an insignificant minority regards the psychic phenomenon
as a category of existence *per se* and draws the necessary conclusions. It is indeed paradoxical that *the* category of existence, the
indispensable *sine qua non* of all existence, namely the psyche,
should be treated as if it were only semi-existent. Psychic existence
is the only category of existence of which we have *immediate*
knowledge, since nothing can be known unless it first appears as a
psychic image.   CW 11, §769

These habits and continuities and daily organizations of personality certainly cannot encompass the definition of consciousness, a mystery that still baffles every area of research. To put it together with ego limits consciousness to the perspectives of the cave which today we would call the literalistic, personalistic, practicalistic, naturalistic, and humanistic fallacies. From the traditional psychology (of Neoplatonism), ego-consciousness does not deserve the name of consciousness at all.

Consciousness arising from soul derives from images and could be called imaginal. According to Jung, the sine qua non of any consciousness whatsoever is the "psychic image."[a] "Every psychic process is an image and an 'imagining,' otherwise no consciousness could exist. . ." (CW 11, §889). On the one hand an image is the inward reflection of an external object. On the other hand, and this is the way Jung prefers to use the word, images are the very stuff of psychic reality. Image is "a concept derived from poetic usage, namely, a figure of fancy or *fantasy-image*" (CW 6, §743). Images are "inner," "archaic," "primordial"; their ultimate source is in the archetypes, and their expression is presented most characteristically in the formulation of myth. Consciousness arising from anima would therefore look to myth, as it manifests in the mythologems of dreams and fantasies and the pattern of lives; whereas ego-consciousness takes its orientations from the literalisms of its perspectives, i.e., that fantasy it defines as "reality."

Because fantasy-images provide the basis of consciousness, we turn to them for basic understanding. "Becoming conscious" would now mean becoming aware of fantasies and the recognition of them *everywhere* and not merely in a 'fantasy world' separate from 'reality.' Especially, we would want to recognize them as they play through that "mirror in which the unconscious becomes aware of its own face" (CW 14, §129), the ego, its thought structures and practical notions of reality. Fantasy-images now become the instrumental mode of perceiving and insighting. By means of them we realize better what Jung so often insisted upon: the psyche is the subject of our perceptions, the perceiver through fantasy, rather than the object of our perceptions. Rather than analyzing fantasies, we analyze by means of them; and translating reality into fantasy-images would better define becoming conscious than would the former notion given by ego of translating fantasy into

realities. "The psyche creates reality every day. The only expression I can use for this activity is *fantasy*" (CW 6, §78).

In particular, the fantasies arising from and giving insight into attachments would refer to anima consciousness. Because anima appears in our affinities, as the *fascinosum* of our attractions and obsessions, where we feel most personal, here this consciousness best mythologizes. It is a consciousness *bound to life*, both at the level of the vital, vegetative soul as it used to be called (the psychosomatic symptom as it is now called) and at the level of involvements of every kind, from petty passions, gossip, to the dilemmas of philosophy. Although consciousness based on anima is inseparable from life, nature, the feminine, as well as from fate and death, it does not follow that this consciousness is naturalistic, or fatalistic, otherworldly and morose, or particularly 'feminine.' It means merely in these realms it turns; these are the metaphors to which it is attached.

Attachment now becomes a more significant term in anima consciousness than do those more guilt-making, and thus ego-referent, terms like commitment, relatedness, and responsibility. In fact, the relativization of the ego means placing in abeyance such metaphors as: choice and light, problem-solving and reality testing, strengthening, developing, controlling, progressing. In their place, as more adequate descriptions of consciousness and its activities, we would use metaphors long familiar to the alchemy of analytical practice: fantasy, image, reflection, insight, and, also, mirroring, holding, cooking, digesting, echoing, gossiping, deepening.

II

... there can be no consciousness
without the perception of differences.

CW 14, §603

THERE are further perceptions of differences in the notion of anima that may help us become more conscious about what we are saying and doing, and even experiencing, in regard to this archetype. Here again I am drawing a distinction between anima as experience, or an *empirical* phenomenology, and anima as notion, or a *critical* phenomenology, utterly convinced that in psychology we cannot make observations about any phenomena without being aware of the ideas by means of which we are making our observations. Ideas that we do not know we have have us. And then they shape our experiences from behind, unbeknown. Psychology's job, it seems to me, is to see the subjective, archetypal factor in our sight, before or while looking at facts and events. Other sciences have to pretend to being objective, to be describing things as they are; psychology fortunately is always bound by its psychic limitations and can be spared the pretense of objectivity. In place of the obligation to be objectively factual, it is obliged to be subjectively aware, which becomes possible only if we are willing to have an exhaustive go at the assumptions in our primary notions.

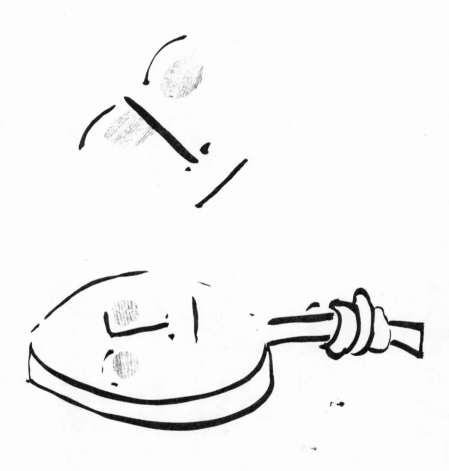

6. Anima and Depersonalization

TOWARD the end of the previous chapter, a group of passages from Jung stressed the difference between anima consciousness and ego consciousness, indicating the reliance of ego upon a factor behind it, the anima. In these passages it is implied that the sense of personal identity is given, not by the ego, but to the ego by the anima. These passages are relevant for understanding that clinical condition called "depersonalization."

Although psychiatry textbooks usually give but a sentence or paragraph to depersonalization (sometimes called derealization), there is, as with everything else, a substantial body of literature on the subject. A collection of basic papers on the theme has been edited by J.-E. Meyer, *Depersonalisation* (Darmstadt: Wissenschaftliche Buchgesellschaft, 1968), the English language chapters having been put into German for the occasion. A plethora of cases serve as examples, and most papers include ample references.

The collection begins with a long paper by Dilthey on the belief in the reality of the external world (*Ges. Schrift.* V, pp. 90–135) and follows with the major study by Paul Schilder (1914), which has provided the basis for most later discussions. Here is Schilder's definition in my translation (Meyer, p. 46*):

> A condition in which an individual feels himself thoroughly changed in regard to his former state of being. This change encompasses both the ego and the external world and results in the individual not recognizing himself as a personality. His actions seem to him automatic. As an onlooker he observes his activities and deeds. The outer world appears alien and new and has lost its reality.

A person says: "I am not I," or "I feel that I am not a person at all."[33]

---

* All page references in this section, unless otherwise indicated, are to *Depersonalisation*.

Bearing in mind the notion of anima, let us review depersonalization's major characteristics. *First,* it is not specific to any syndrome. It is reported in toxic states, epilepsy, and organic brain diseases, as well as in normals, in puberty as well as in old age, and* in hysteria, melancholia, anxiety states, neurotic phobias and compulsions, as well as in both schizophrenia and manic-depressive psychoses. It has no standard span of time, sometimes of long duration, sometimes ephemeral. It seems to be central and general, not peripheral; brain-oriented authors try to localize it. *Second,* many authors have conceived depersonalization as a disturbance of the ego–world relationship, particularly the relationship which constitutes the sense of reality of both: the depersonalized individual feels not only that he is not real but also that the world is not real. It is behind a veil or a glass wall; there and not really there. *Third,* it is said to occur particularly in situations of monotony, apathy, routine, with a poverty of sensory input. Experiences become mere events and no longer mean "me" (*Meinhaftigkeit,* K. Schneider, pp. 256–59). *Fourth,* following Janet, the type of personality that shows the symptom is the asthenic or psychasthenic. It belongs to psychic lability, what we would today call insecure, vague, spaced out. This type did not disappear with Janet but seems to exist today in a group reported by M. Roth (1960). These are young men scarcely turned twenty, compulsive neurotics and introverted worriers who are also highly intelligent and can portray fascinating descriptions of their depersonalization experiences. Roth (p. 380) finds depersonalization rarely in women and then in connection with hysteria.* *Fifth,* together with the emptying of "I," there is a transformation of world: it loses its aesthetic, physiognomic, and empathic character. It is no longer personally significant; there is no "importance" in A. N. Whitehead's sense. There is a loss of time value, of depth perception and visual perspective. Here and there, near and far merge; the world becomes flatland (B. Kimura, 1963, p. 394).

Schilder shows that the depersonalized experience does *not* depend on any of the usual functions of ego consciousness: memory, perception, association, feeling, thinking, willing. These all remain intact, but their intention and vitality are relativized by an in-

* On the relation of hysteria and the Kore anima figure, see Niel Micklem, "On Hysteria: The Mythical Syndrome," *Spring 1974,* pp. 147–65.

(a) The richness of the human psyche and its essential character are probably determined by this reflective instinct. CW 8, §242

Through reflection, "life" and its "soul" are abstracted from Nature and endowed with a separate existence. (reflection is a spiritual act that runs counter to the natural process; ... it should, therefore, be understood as an act of *becoming conscious.*)
CW 11, §235 (and n9)

(b) ... sulphur is the soul ... of all living things; ... it is equated with "nostra anima" (our soul).... Paracelsus likewise calls sulphur the soul. CW 14, §136

The green colour attributed to Sulphur he has in common with Venus.... CW 14, §140n124

(c) ... permanent loss of the anima means.... resignation, weariness, sloppiness, irresponsibility.... CW 9, i, §147

dependent factor that has been called the "personal co-efficient" (p. 118). Indeed, depersonalization abstracts the ego to its barest dictionary definition: "the individual's experience of himself."[34] All the functions of consciousness, including ego itself, are there and working, but the personal sense of being, subjective interiority, the sense of "me-ness," is gone, and with this absence is lost too the sense of world. Gebsattel (p. 244) sees in this loss and absence an existential "void" and "abyss."

These salient features of depersonalization are relevant to our pursuit of anima. According to Jung, it is the anima who provides the relationship between man and world as well as between man and his interior subjectivity. She is in fact the personification of that interiority and subjectivity, the very sense of personality: "man derives his human personality . . . his consciousness of himself as a personality . . . primarily from the influence of quasi-personal archetypes" (CW 5, §388). But it is particularly the anima archetype which makes possible experience *as personal* as we saw in chapter five, "Anima and Psyche."

As we saw there, too, anima refers to the reflexive instinct which Jung associates with the basis of consciousness;[a] and he defines her as archetype of life, as the personification which unconsciously involves us with larger collectivities of both inner and outer worlds. In this sense Jung frequently speaks of anima as the projection-making factor, the Shakti and the Maya that gives life to a person. In alchemy, the active effulgence of sulphur can represent anima[b] as can green, color of nature, hope, and life (chapter two).

The condition can be distinguished from depression since depersonalization is less the inhibition of vital functions and the narrowing of focus than it is a loss of personal involvement with and attachment to self and world. There seems another archetype at work than in depression. As Roth noted with his young men, there is a curious ability to observe one's condition coupled with morbid introspection by the ego in search of soul. We each may have experienced depersonalization and derealization in less extreme degree. I refer to those states of apathy, monotony, dryness, and weary resignation, the sense of not caring and of not believing in one's value, that nothing is important or all is voided, outside and inside. Jung attributes states such as these to the anima archetype.[c] We might see this now less as a "negative" anima state than as a

105

mild depersonalization, a loss of soul, or what Jung calls (CW 9, i, §147) "permanent loss of the anima."

Loss of anima is familiar at the end of a love-affair. There is a loss of vitality and reality, not only about the other person, the affair, and love but also in regard to oneself and the very world itself. "Nothing seems real anymore." "I feel dead, empty, mechanical like a robot." It happens in men and women: Demeter's lost soul, when Kore is captured by an invisible dark power, brings the whole world of nature to a stop.

One passage from Jung is especially relevant to Schilder's idea of the missing personal co-efficient. About the anima Jung says (CW 9, i, §57):

> It is a "factor" in the proper sense of the word. Man cannot make it; on the contrary, it is always the *a priori* element in his moods, reactions, impulses, and whatever else is spontaneous in psychic life. It is something that lives of itself, that makes us live; it is a life behind consciousness that cannot be completely integrated with it, but from which, on the contrary, consciousness arises.

This statement accords with the notion of *anima* in Roman Latin,[35] where *anima* connoted a breath soul, a generative force in the head, associated with one's individual *genius* (or personal *daimon* in the Greek sense). *Anima* did not refer to the specific functions of consciousness (thinking, willing, perceiving, feeling, etc.), nor did it refer to the registration of experiences (attention), functions, and activities that later became ego. Anima meant something deeper than that and thus was a term, much like the early Greek *psyché* and the Egyptian *ba*, that also referred to soul apart from life (in relation with death). *Anima* was the deeper generic force behind specific conscious functions in life, much as Jung describes it in the above passage. An absence of anima would affect less the functions of consciousness than the personal *genius* or *daimon* (now technically called "the personal co-efficient").

Depersonalization presents a striking similarity with what anthropology has called "loss of soul." And in fact "depersonalization" is "also used of a philosophy of the universe, which no longer regards natural forces as manifestations of supernatural agents or

(a) The anima is nothing but a representation of the personal nature of the autonomous system in question.   CW 13, §61

gods."[36] Loss of anima means both the loss of internal animation and external animism.

As I tried to present in my Terry Lecture "Personifying,"[37] the native habit of the soul to personify is the ground of animism, anthropomorphism, and the personifications of language, poetry, and myth; it is the ground of dreams and of our experience of divine figures. Our sense of personality, attachment to persons, beliefs in personal immortality, and our cult of personal relationships and development – all rest upon personifying, which in turn is an effect of the anima archetype.

Absence of anima opens one to the soul's immeasurable depths, that primary characteristic of the psyche according to Herakleitos,[38] revealing those depths as an abyss. Not only is the guide and the bridge gone, but so too is the possibility of a personal connection through personified representations. For it is through anima that the autonomous systems of the psyche are experienced in personified form.[a] Without her the depths become a void, as the existentialist von Gebsattel says. This happens because the anima who "personifies the collective unconscious" (CW 10, §714 and other passages listed below in chapter eight) is not there to mediate the depths in personified images with personal intentions. At the same time, the world outside is perceived without its depths, losing perspective, becoming a soulless flatland.

This loss is not merely a psychiatric condition; it is also a cosmology. We all live to a larger extent than we realize in the state of depersonalization. Hence the work with anima – including my writing and your reading – because it is at the same time a work on the moribund *anima mundi*, is a noble task. The self-knowledge that depth psychology offers is not enough if the depths of the world soul are neglected. A self-knowledge that rests within a cosmology which declares the mineral, vegetable, and animal world beyond the human person to be impersonal and inanimate is not only inadequate. It is also delusional. No matter how well we may know ourselves, we remain walking, talking ghosts, cosmologically set apart from the other beings of our milieu. From Plato through the alchemists on whom Jung leans, and for Jung himself, it was not the personal anima alone that counted but also the *anima mundi* (CW 8, §393). The work on one's own person aims to open the senses and the heart to the life and beauty of an animated

(a)   The gods have become diseases. . . .   CW 13, §54

world. Jung's philosophical position of being in soul, restated elsewhere as not the psyche is in man but man is in the psyche, maintains the ancient connection and the ancient concern with *anima
mundi*; and Jung's animated sense of things at Bollingen presents
this position as his *Lebensphilosophie*. Even his conceptual writing
that requires animated ideas such as shadow, trickster, or wise old
man protects his thought from the depersonalized, soulless flatland of academic psychology. Wherever he speaks of soul and anima he never yields the ambiguity, thereby maintaining against the
Luciferian temptation of enlightenment through severance which
would sharply distinguish the processes within my intimate soul
and those of the *anima mundi*, resulting in singleness of meaning,
Newton's sleep.

In sum, if the essence of depersonalization can be condensed into an absence of the personal co-efficient, I believe we have located
the missing person in anima – but found it in notion only. How to
recapture it in therapy is another matter.

But where to look tells us something about how to look. By
relating archetype and symptom we have an inkling at which altar
to place the complaint – there are Gods in our diseases, suggests
Jung,[a] and so we can relate our disease to them. Relating the anima archetype to the depersonalization symptom could take place
by revivifying images. In a somewhat similar condition where "the
patient's world had become cold, empty, and grey," Jung turned to
fantasy because: "Libido can never be apprehended except in a
definite form; that is to say, it is identical with fantasy-images"
(CW 7, §345). Imagination is the particular province of the anima:
"image *is* psyche" says Jung (CW 13, §75). (This relation between
anima and fantasy we discussed in chapter five, and the relation
between soul and imagination has been a theme in articles by
Casey, Corbin, Durand, Whitmont, and Woolger in issues of the
Spring annual during the early '70s.)

The revivification of images reconstructs personal belief through
belief in a personified world with personal intentions and confidence in oneself as a carrier of interior personalities. Grinnell
(*Spring 1970*) has described this as "psychological faith." As he

111

(a)   Instead of allowing himself [Western man] to be convinced once more that the daemon is an illusion, he ought to experience once more the reality of this illusion.... His dissociative tendencies are actual psychic personalities possessing a differential reality.... The personification enables us to see the relative reality of the autonomous system, and not only makes its assimilation possible but also depotentiates the daemonic forces of life.   CW 13, §55

The light that gradually dawns on him [modern man] consists in his understanding that his fantasy is a real psychic process which is happening to him personally.... But if you recognize your own involvement you yourself must enter into the process with your personal reactions, just as if you were one of the fantasy figures, or rather, as if the drama being enacted before your eyes were real. It is a psychic fact that this fantasy is happening, and it is as real as you – as a psychic entity – are real. If this crucial operation is not carried out, all the changes are left to the flow of images, and you yourself remain unchanged.   CW 14, §753

For decades I always turned to the anima when I felt that my emotional behavior was disturbed, and that something had been constellated in the unconscious. I would then ask the anima: "Now what are you up to? What do you see? I should like to know." After some resistance she regularly produced an image. As soon as the image was there, the unrest or sense of oppression vanished. The whole energy of these emotions was transformed into interest in and curiosity about the image. I would speak with the anima about the images she communicated to me....   MDR, pp. 187–88

shows in the case of Jung – his dream of the little girl and the dove – faith in psyche and in oneself as personality is a particular effect of anima. Anima has this effect through the presentation of images, i.e., in Jung's case, as Grinnell shows, after the break-up with Freud and the break-down in Jung, Jung became Jung through his encounter with imagination. The vivification of images led to his psychological faith, his personal psychological position, and his sense of personality. But any therapeutic method for restoring an animated, repersonalized world must constellate – and in the therapist himself – the sense of utter reality of the personified image.[a]

(a) ... the autonomous complex of anima and animus is essentially a psychological function that has usurped, or rather retained, a "personality" only because this function is itself autonomous and undeveloped. But already we can see how it is possible to break up the personifications, since by making them conscious we convert them into bridges to the unconscious. It is because we are not using them purposefully as functions that they remain personified complexes. So long as they are in this state they must be accepted as relatively independent personalities. They cannot be integrated into consciousness while their contents remain unknown. The purpose of the dialectical process is to bring these contents into the light; and only when this task has been completed, and the conscious mind has become sufficiently familiar with the unconscious processes reflected in the anima, will the anima be felt simply as a function.

CW 7, §339

To the degree that the patient takes an active part, the personified figure of anima or animus will disappear. It becomes the function of relationship between conscious and unconscious.

CW 7, §370

... the immediate goal has been achieved, namely the conquest of the anima as an autonomous complex, and her transformation into a function of relationship between the conscious and the unconscious..

CW 7, §374

The immediate goal of the analysis of the unconscious, therefore, is to reach a state where the unconscious contents no longer remain unconscious and no longer express themselves indirectly as animus and anima phenomena; that is to say, a state in which animus and anima become functions of relationship to the unconscious.... With that the anima phenomenon comes to a stop.

CW 7, §387

7. Integration of the Anima

ONE OF Jung's many passages may lead us to believe that at some point personifying comes to an end and is even a desired end. The implication is clear: integration into consciousness means converting the person into a function.[a] It also means moving from image to content, from the sensate immediacy of fantasies to the psychology of meanings. For anima presents herself in fantasies, rather than meanings. It is implied that the anima as function is superior to the anima personified. Further support for anima integration as "breaking up the personifications" can be drawn from other

(a) The dissolution of the anima means that we have gained insight into the driving forces of the unconscious, but not that we have made these forces ineffective. CW 7, §391

(b) It is not we who personify them [unconscious figures]; they have a personal nature from the very beginning. Only when this is thoroughly recognized can we think of depersonalizing them, of "subjugating the anima".... CW 13, §62

(c) The unconscious anima is a creature without relationships, an autoerotic being whose one aim is to take total possession of the individual. CW 16, §504

His mistress appears before him . . . seeming to him like a goddess in heaven. The repressed erotic impression has activated the latent primordial image of the goddess, i.e., the archetypal soul-image.

Through insight into the actual existence of his erotic desire, Hermas was able to acknowledge this metaphysical reality. The sensual libido . . . now passed to his soul-image and invested it with the reality which the object had claimed exclusively for itself. Consequently his soul could speak to good effect and successfully enforce her demands. CW 6, §§383–87

(d) After the middle of life, however, permanent loss of the anima means a diminution of vitality, of flexibility, and of human kindness. The result, as a rule, is premature rigidity, crustiness, stereotypy, fanatical one-sidedness, obstinacy, pedantry, or else resignation, weariness, sloppiness, irresponsibility, and finally a childish *ramollissement* with a tendency to alcohol. CW 9, i, §147

passages where Jung speaks of "the dissolution of the anima"[a] and of "depersonalizing" and "subjugating the anima."[b] See also CW 16, §504 and the long discussion of Hermas with his Rhoda (CW 6, §381 ff.) and the early Christian struggle with sexuality evoked by the anima.[c]

The notion of anima integration in the long passage cited above (CW 7, §339), and elsewhere (CW 7, §374), has a heroic tinge; its formulation is in the language of "conquest," battle, darkness and light. The process is described in the ego language of compensation with a moralistic undertone ("because we are not using them purposefully as functions . . . they remain personified complexes," CW 7, §339). Consequently, we have that antagonism of "masculine ego versus the feminine 'other,' i.e., conscious versus unconscious personified as anima" (CW 16, §434). The entire relationship with anima is placed into the mythologem of the heroic ego and his archetypal fight with the dragon. Then efforts to integrate, "to bring these contents to light," become a depotentiating of personifications and of their imaginal power, a drying-up of the waters, and a slaying of the angel (seen to be a dangerous fairy-demon by the ego), whose real purpose is to individualize itself within a personal relation to an individual. This Corbin has pointed out.[39] The feminine image that the hero meets is his guardian angel, not his enemy, and it is *her* individualization, not his or mine, that matters to the soul. Her individualization into distinct personality is precisely what soul-making is all about. To depersonify anima – if this is truly possible at all – would serve only one psychological purpose: to keep the ego forever in its heroic stance.

Depersonalizing the anima can produce unnecessary damage in human affairs when this idea is taken literally, leading to brutal rejection (presented as noble renunciations) and a subsequent "diminution of vitality, of flexibility, and of human kindness" in a series of psychic horrors Jung goes on to recount in the same paragraph.[d] The entire operation of literal choice between spirit and body, inner and outer, positive and negative has its source in 'ego consciousness' which maintains itself best through giving reality to these fantasies, forcing opposition between them, suppressing one, and then calling this game 'choice.' So the anima always presents heroic consciousness with a moral dilemma. But the moral dilemma is in the nature of the ego and not in the nature of the anima.

117

(a) ... for the archetypes are universal and belong to the collective psyche over which the ego has no control. Thus animus and anima are images representing archetypal figures which mediate between consciousness and the unconscious. Though they can be made conscious they cannot be integrated into the ego-personality, since as archetypes they are also autonomous.

2 January 1957, Letter to Anonymous

(b) I have defined the anima as a personification of the unconscious in general, and have taken it as a bridge to the unconscious. ... If the unconscious figures are not acknowledged as spontaneous agents, we become victims of a one-sided belief in the power of consciousness. ...

CW 13, §62

(c) Together they [the anima and animus] form a divine pair, one of whom ... is ... rather like Hermes ... while the other ... wears the features of Aphrodite, Helen (Selene), Persephone, and Hecate. Both of them are unconscious powers, "gods" in fact. ...

CW 9, ii, §41

To the men of antiquity the anima appeared as a goddess or a witch, while for medieval man the goddess was replaced by the Queen of Heaven and Mother Church.   CW 9, i, §61

(d) It is not we who personify them; they have a personal nature from the very beginning. Only when this is thoroughly recognized can we think of depersonalizing them, of "subjugating the anima". ...

CW 13, §62

Consciousness can only exist through continual recognition of the unconscious. ...   CW 9, i, §178

(e) ... Michael Maier's journey to the seven mouths of the Nile. ... is a description of the dreamer's ascent to a world of gods and heroes, of his initiation into a Venus mystery. ...   CW 14, §297

When we read the major passage with which we began this section in the light of others on the same theme, we discover more precisely what "integration" means. "Though the effects of anima and animus can be made conscious, they themselves are factors transcending consciousness and beyond the reach of perception and volition. Hence they remain autonomous despite the integration of their contents" (CW 9, ii, §40).[a] All we can do is remember their spontaneous reality behind contents, projections, effects[b] and grant "relative autonomy and reality" to these psychic "figures" (CW 9, ii, §44), which Jung often presents as Gods and Goddesses.[c] Anima "integration" is thus "knowledge of this structure," a recognition of her as archetype (CW 14, §616). The operative term is thorough *recognition*.[d] And just what is to be recognized? – the relatively autonomous, personified nature of the archetype. From this it would seem that anima integration means just the reverse of turning personification into function and that, by continuing to recognize her as a relatively independent person, we are indeed performing the work of integration.

The question as answered by alchemy is no longer simply a disjunction: either figure or function, person or process. The personal image of anima is necessary for performing certain functions and constellating certain contents. Without the personal image (e.g., Michael Maier's *imaginatio*)[e] we would not be led (seduced) or interested (tempted); we would not experience certain qualities (the bitterness of salt, a personified substance); we could not experience the endogamous libido (incest with the soror); we would not find the delight and delusion in the dissolving, coloring, and whitening.

Consequently, the "depersonalizing" of anima (CW 13, §62) may mean depriving the anima of her *personalistic effects* and projec-

119

(a) Melusina, the deceptive Shakti. . . . should no longer dance before the adept with alluring gestures, but must become what she was from the beginning: a part of his wholeness. As such she must be "conceived in the mind." CW 13, §223

The "mother" corresponds to the "virgin anima," who is not turned towards the outer world and is therefore not corrupted by it. She is turned rather towards the "inner sun". . . . CW 5, §464

(b) Recognizing the shadow is what I call the apprenticepiece, but making out with the anima is the masterpiece which not many can bring off. 9 February 1959, Letter to Traugott Egloff

tions, but *not* of her appearance to the interior sense as a *personified numen*.[a] The "'internalization through sacrifice'" (CW 16, §438), which seems Jung's method for working through the "Meisterstück"[b] of anima integration does not require dissolving her as a personified figure.

Internalization through sacrifice – the principal concern of chapters VII and VIII of *Symbols of Transformation* (CW 5) and of Jung's theory of transference (CW 16), in fact, the latent program throughout the process of individuation (CW 12 and 14) – takes on a far subtler meaning. This internalization and this sacrifice cannot be conceived as suppression of the extraverted soul or as sublimation (raising something lower to a more noble condition). It is not an immolation but a consecration. Sacrifice takes on its original sense of returning some event in the human world to the Gods, thereby raising the *value* (not the substance) of that event; and where internalizing means working into the interior of that event so that its value, and thus its sacredness, appears to insight. And, curiously, what appears during this sacrificial procedure called "internalization" and what enables insight to happen at all is the personified voice or figure of an anima.

The crucial support for my understanding of anima integration to mean *recognition of the anima as personified numen* comes from Jung himself:

> There are no conclusive arguments against the hypothesis that these archetypal figures are endowed with personality at the outset and are not just secondary personalizations. In so far as the archetypes do not represent mere functional relationships, they manifest themselves as *daimones,* as personal agencies. In this form they are felt as actual experiences and are not "figments of the imagination," as rationalism would have us believe. (CW 5, §388) . . . instead of deriving these figures from our psychic conditions, [we] must derive our psychic conditions from these figures. (CW 13, §299) It is not we who personify them; they have a personal nature from the very beginning. (ibid., §62) [It] . . . is quite right to treat the anima as an autonomous personality. . . . (CW 7, §322; cf. §§317–27)

This personal nature is experienced in and through personified images. To leave these behind leaves the archetype itself, since ar-

121

chetypes are personified a priori, "at the outset." Therefore, "internalization through sacrifice" must mean something other than "depersonalizing." Does it mean moving the anima image from outer person to inner person, i.e., withdrawing the projections from a human being?

Here we take an excursion to consider those wrangles in therapy about anima projections in love relationships. Sometimes one feels in Jung a *horror animae,* as when he says "marriage with the anima" is "possible only in the complete absence of psychological self-knowledge" (CW 16, §433). Here I believe it is the literalization against which he warns and not the actuality of anima lived in life. It is yet to be established that we find a truer and more authentic relationship with soul by dispensing with its living carrier in concrete existence. To break off a complex-ridden relationship charged with anima projections would be to literalize her into the person carrying the projections. Every prescription or proscription concerning what to do or how to behave literalizes. This is as true for actions in the "inner" world as for the "outer." Internalizing can become just as literal as acting out.

Whenever internalization through sacrifice means putting the knife to concrete life because it is concrete – e.g., renouncing "marriage with the anima," or sexuality, or tangible fascinations for the sake of the self's individuation process – then there has been no internalization whatsoever, merely a more radical literalization. Instead of internalization through sacrifice, there is literalization through suppression. Then, sacrifice itself has been literalized as denying, cutting, or killing concrete life, and internalization has been placed literally "inside" one's head or skin. (This primitive or Philistine[40] notion of internality was reviewed in chapter five above.) Likewise externality is not 'out there' in the concrete, extraverted world. It refers to the evident, obvious, prima facie, or superficial aspect of all events ("inner" or "outer"). We fall into externality all the time, even when internalizing in active imagination, taking the figures at face value, listening to their counsel literally, or simply by having to do active imagination at all in order to find depth, interiority, fantasy, and anima. Then the world of psychic images and the anima figure within this world hold magic sway. One is in thrall to Mistress Soul. No matter how introvertedly performed, this is externality, acting in, literalism, absolutiz-

(a) Prometheus surrenders himself . . . to his soul, that is, to the function of relation to the inner world. . . . Prometheus concedes her an absolute significance, as mistress and guide. . . . He sacrifices his individual ego to the soul, to the relation with the unconscious as the matrix of eternal images and meanings. . . . Prometheus loses all connection with the surrounding world, and hence also the very necessary corrective offered by external reality.   CW 6, §278

(b) . . . it is readily understandable that the primordial image of the hermaphrodite should reappear in modern psychology in the guise of the male-female antithesis, in other words as *male* consciousness and personified *female* unconsciousness. . . .

Originally this archetype played its part entirely in the field of fertility magic and thus remained . . . a purely biological phenomenon. . . . But even in early antiquity the symbolical meaning of the act seems to have increased. . . . and natural philosophy turned it into an abstract *theoria*. These developments meant the gradual transformation of the archetype into a psychological process which, in theory, we can call a combination of conscious and unconscious processes.   CW 9, i, §§296–97

ing, or whatever else one likes to call it. Jung gives an example of it in Spitteler's Prometheus.[a]

This obtuse sort of literalism also affects the notion of the hermaphrodite, as if it were simply a matter of joining the characteristics of two genders in one person. A man attempts to become more feminine, feeling and 'eros-connected' with the aim of integrating the anima – a notion of anima which we have already tried to dispel in earlier chapters. All the while that he is performing this *imitatio animae*, he is actually becoming more literal than imaginal and metaphorical which is what anima consciousness more likely implies. As Jung shows all through the *Mysterium Coniunctionis* (CW 14) and elsewhere, "male" and "female" are biological metaphors for the psychic conditions of conscious and unconscious.[b] Anima integration in the model of the hermaphrodite does not mean acquiring characteristics of the other gender; rather, it means a double consciousness, mercurial, true and untrue, action and inaction, sight and blindness, living the impossible oxymoron, more like an animal who is at once superbly conscious in its actions and utterly unconscious of them. To take the freakish image of the hermaphrodite and literalize it into sexual genders and then moralize it into a bi-sexual goal for behavior is a move as mistaken as considering the phallus to be the biological penis or the great mother to be one's own mother of one's childhood. The battle over literalism is never won; it simply reappears in new guises – thereby forcing us to be psychological.

It is not persons that we sacrifice but the personal. Now the several questions of this chapter come to one issue. Internalizing through sacrifice has nothing to do with choices between outer and inner. Such is literalism. Nor has it anything to do with depersonalizing in either form: changing personifications into functions and contents or transmigrations of soul from outer persons to inner images.

Depersonalizing the anima means what it says: *seeing through the personal aspects* of all personifications. It refers to that recognition that all the personal me-ness and self-important subjectivity derive from an archetype that is quite impersonal. Precisely this

(a) As I see it, the psyche is a world in which the ego is contained.

CW 13, §75

You rightly emphasize that man in my view is enclosed in *the* psyche (not in *his* psyche).

14 May 1950, Letter to Joseph Goldbrunner

connection between the personal and the archetype of the personal both depersonalizes and is sacrifice. For sacrifice, as we all know and always forget, means just this sort of connecting personal human events with their impersonal divine background. It means seeing the anima archetype in what's personally going on – and wherever it's going on, both with outer anima persons and inner anima images. The personal aspects of inner images, too, need seeing through as relatively autonomous archetypal events. They are impersonal and not concerned with "me" on the level of my subjective importance. Conversations with the inner anima image and her actions in dreams can make "me" anima-ridden just as any involvement with outer anima persons.

By returning the infusions, the beauty, the wiles, and vanities to their origins in the Goddesses, giving it all back to its background, we depersonalize the entire compulsive, autonomous performance. Then we can acknowledge that definition: "The anima is nothing but a representation of the personal nature of the autonomous system in question" (CW 13, §61).

Integrating the anima, which means becoming an integer or one with her, could only take place by our remembrance that we are already in her. Human being is being-in-soul (*esse in anima*) from the beginning. Integration is thus a shift of viewpoint from her in me to me in her. "Man is in *the* psyche (not in *his* psyche),"[a] which we also discussed in chapter five above. This recognition of where we actually and ontologically are is a sacrifice of our habitual consciousness, internalizing it within the embrace of the wider notion of psyche. This too is an "internalization through sacrifice" which can be spoken of more accurately as "relativizing the ego" (above, pp. 91–93) than as "integrating the anima."

(a) The anima personifies the collective unconscious. . . .

CW 10, §714

. . . the unconscious is often personified by the anima. . . .

CW 11, §107

I have defined the anima as a personification of the unconscious.

CW 9, ii, §20n1

(b) I have defined the anima as a personification of the unconscious in general, and have taken it as a bridge to the unconscious, in other words, as a function of relationship to the unconscious.

CW 13, §62

. . . by making them [anima and animus] conscious we convert them into bridges to the unconscious. CW 7, §339

. . . *anima* . . . is the personification of the inferior functions which relate a man to the collective unconscious. CW 18, §187

. . . the anima is the image of the subject in his relation to the collective unconscious. . . . CW 7, §521

8. *Mediatrix of the Unknown*

LET US now turn to three further and closely allied definitions: 1) anima personifies the collective unconscious;[a] 2) anima is
the function of relationship to the unconscious;[b] 3) anima is medi-

(a) X. is undoubtedly the anima, representing the coll.[ective] unc.
[onscious].
>   24 December 1931, Letter to Count Hermann Keyserling

. . . mostly it is the anima who in singular or plural form represents
the collective unconscious.   CW 14, §128

. . . encounter with the anima logically leads to a great expansion
of our sphere of experience. The anima is a representative of the
unconscious and hence a mediatrix. . . .
>   13 March 1958, Anonymous

. . . the anima plays the role of the mediatrix between the unconscious and the conscious. . . .   CW 10, §715

The anima mediates between consciousness and the collective unconscious. . . .   CW 14, §498n381

. . . soul is a life-giving daemon who plays his elfin game above and
below human existence. . . .   CW 9, i, §56

(b) . . . the figure of the unknown woman is a personification of the
unconscious, which I have called the "anima."   CW 16, §17

(c) At the top of the whole picture is the personification of the unconscious, a naked anima-figure who turns her back. That is a typical
position; in the beginning of the objectivation of these images the
anima-figure often turns her back.   CW 18, §412

(d) When projected, the anima always has a feminine form with definite characteristics. This empirical finding does not mean that the
archetype is constituted like that *in itself*.   CW 9, i, §142

atrix of the unknown,[a] acts as psychopompos to the unknown, and appears herself as unknown.[b]

These definitions refer to the phenomenology of "unknownness" which we have been noticing throughout – anima as innocent, empty, vague, white (or dark); the smoke, mist, and opacity; her elusive, enigmatic, obscurantist behavior; her dubious, shady origins or her associations with remote history or alien culture; the images of her turning her back,[c] or veiled, or hidden, or incarcerated in the darkness of primal matter. Or she is unknown as the projection-maker and illusion-maker. The unknown also subsumes the phenomenology of sudden unwilled moods and attractions that come without reason and go just as inexplicably. Finally, anima is the unknown as the mystery of consciousness in its relation with nature and life.

It is this *fundamental unconsciousness* of the archetype – absence of light, morality, meaning, conflict, intention, historical time, and cultural image – that Jung points to in some passages about the "unknown" nature of the anima. For the anima's "irruption into consciousness often amounts to a psychosis." "Unlike other contents, they [anima and animus] always remain strangers to the world of consciousness, unwelcome intruders saturating the atmosphere with uncanny forebodings or even with the fear of madness." "They [anima and animus] undoubtedly belong to the material that comes to light in schizophrenia" (CW 9,i, §§517–20). He also suggests that anima "might explain the very much greater number of suicides among men" (CW 10, §79).

So when Jung says the archetypes are unknowable I do not believe he means merely that their theoretical structure is beyond the possibility of knowledge. I do not believe he is here speaking of the anima archetype only as a Kantian noumenon, an unknowable potential, a hypothetical conjecture.[d] He is speaking both epistemologically and phenomenally, empirically: the unconscious psyche cannot altogether be known. That is what "unconscious" means: both unknown *and* unknowable. What is unknown can become known, but what is unknowable remains fundamentally and always unable to be known; and it is precisely this psychic unconsciousness, beyond the reach of insight and knowledge, that the anima mediates. She makes us unconscious. As she is the very cra-

(a) In elfin nature wisdom and folly appear as one and the same; and
they *are* one and the same as long as they are acted out by the anima. Life is crazy and meaningful at once.   CW 9,i, §65

... the anima emerges in exemplary fashion from the primeval
slime, laden with all the pulpy and monstrous appendages of the
deep.   13 August 1931, Letter to Count Hermann Keyserling

When such a fate [Nekyia] befalls a man ... he usually encounters
the unconscious in the form of the "Dark One," a Kundry of horri-
bly grotesque, primeval ugliness or else of infernal beauty. In
Faust's metamorphosis, Gretchen, Helen, Mary, and the abstract
"Eternal Feminine" correspond to the four female figures of the
Gnostic underworld, Eve, Helen, Mary, and Sophia.

CW 15, §211

(b) Atrophy of feeling is a characteristic of modern man and always
shows itself as a reaction when there is too much feeling around,
and in particular too much false feeling.   CW 15, §183

(c) Everything the anima touches becomes numinous – unconditional,
dangerous, taboo, magical.... She affords the most convincing
reasons for not prying into the unconscious, an occupation that
would break down our moral inhibitions and unleash forces that
had better been left unconscious and undisturbed.

CW 9,i, §59

ziness of life,[a] she drives us crazy. "With the archetype of the anima we enter the realm of the gods. . . . Everything the anima touches becomes numinous – unconditional, dangerous, taboo, magical" (CW 9,i, §59).

Sentimentalities in analytical practice forget this "psychotic" aspect, so taken – that is, mistaken – is practice with the eros and relatedness of anima. Remember: her personalizing, subjectivity, and sensitivity are all *archetypal* qualities; they need sifting through by the feeling function and deliteralizing. Else one takes over these qualities, identifies with them, believing that, by becoming more intimately personal, deeply subjective, and sensitive, one is, again, "integrating the anima," whereas one has let her catch one's feeling, making it false by making it into an imitation of hers. The *imitatio animae* shows first in pseudo-subjectivity, -sensitivity, and -depth. Because she is archetypal she enlarges the dimension of this feeling; it's over-rich, over-refined, and it smells. *Vox populi* calls it hokey.

This infiltration of feeling by anima is how practice gets suborned by one of her clever duplicities: the absence of human feeling in the anima archetype is precisely that which she covers with sentimentalities about herself. But she is her own cure; for, her cold and crazed aspect, La Belle Dame Sans Merci, brings an archetypal correction to her own sentimentality.[41,b]

So let us not imagine anima bridging and mediating inward only as a sibylline benefactrice, teaching us about all the things we did not know, the girl guide whose hand we hold. This is a one-way trip, and there is another direction to her movement. She would also "unleash forces"[c] of the collective unconscious, for across her bridge roll fantasies, projections, emotions that make a person's consciousness unconscious and collective. She makes us like everyone else, mouthing the same clichés, chasing the same ephemera, clinging to the same needs. As mediatrix to the eternally unknowable she is the bridge *both* over the river into the trees *and* into the sludge and quicksand, making the known ever more unknown. The deeper we descend into her ontology, the more opaque consciousness becomes. Then to follow her we must declare like the alchemists that understanding moves from the known to the unknown in an epistemology based upon the dictum *ignotum per ignotius*. Anima explanations point to the unconscious and make us

(a) . . . the first encounter with her usually leads one to infer anything rather than wisdom. This aspect appears only to the person who gets to grips with her seriously. Only then . . . does he come to realize more and more that behind all her cruel sporting with human fate there lies something like a hidden purpose which seems to reflect a superior knowledge of life's laws. It is just the most unexpected, the most terrifyingly chaotic things which reveal a deeper meaning. And the more this meaning is recognized, the more the anima loses her impetuous and compulsive character.

CW 9, i, §64

(b) The anima no longer crosses our path as a goddess, but, it may be as an intimately personal misadventure, or perhaps as our best venture. When, for instance, a highly esteemed professor in his seventies abandons his family and runs off with a young red-headed actress. . . . This is how daemonic power reveals itself to us.

CW 9, i, §62

(c) In his quest for wholeness . . . Michael Maier . . . has found the animal soul and the sibylline anima, who now counsels him to journey to the seven mouths of the Nile. . . .   CW 14, §287

The sibyl, the guide of souls. . . .   CW 14, §300

Our author was led in the first place by the anima-sibyl to undertake the journey through the planetary houses. . . .

CW 14, §313

But a conscious attitude that renounces its ego-bound intentions . . . and submits to the suprapersonal decrees of fate, can claim to be serving a king. This more exalted attitude raises the status of the anima from that of a temptress to a psychopomp.

CW 14, §540

The anima . . . now appears as the psychopomp, the one who shows the way. . . .   CW 12, §74

more unconscious. She mystifies, produces sphinx-like riddles, prefers the cryptic and occult where she can remain hidden: she insists upon uncertainty. By leading whatever is known from off its solid footing, she carries every question into deeper waters, which is also a way of soul-making.

The deeper we follow her, the more fantastic consciousness becomes.[a] Then in dreams she reveals herself as psychotic, a wraith with queer eyes, an "inmate" of my nightly asylum. Union with anima also means union with my psychosis, my fear of madness, my suicide. This conjunction with its sweet sentimentalities is purged by her salt, for it is a conjunction with the craziness of life that is at the same time my own craziness, mediated and personalized through her bringing home a "me" that is an oddity, peculiar and mine, or what Jung calls self.

Analytical psychology in lesser hands than Jung's sometimes lets slip these implications of the unknown. By ruses of lunar or matriarchal consciousness, psychologists sometimes suggest that the obscurity of anima states is not real menace, not real darkness, but a light of another kind. It is as if analytical practice, living out its wise old man fantasy, must cling to the sweet anima at all costs, for this milk-giving daughter is inherent to the senex mythologem so dominant in the analyst. He depends on her help, so he must see her as helpful. Then mediatrix means only mediation and *harmonia* only harmony. These comforting positions are another of the ways anima befuddles thought with her gentle persuasion, protecting herself by preventing us from seeing through to her demonic depths.[b] After all, the reconciling go-between is also that which comes between and, as Jung points out, the cross-cousin kinship marriage with my soul also crosses up my plans, finally becoming the cross of soul. Thus "the encounter with anima and animus means conflict" (CW 16, §470), which is also a pattern of relating with the collective unconscious. Nothing mediates unconsciousness and collectivity better than confusion, rage, and suffering. Harmonia in myth is the daughter of War, and *harmonia* in philosophy (Herakleitos, frgs. 44, 45, 47, 59, 62 – Burnet)[42] is inseparable from strife and discord.

When anima is defined as mediating psychopomp,[c] we are obliged to inquire precisely what is her style of guidance and precisely to what state she takes one, since the soul has other guides. There

135

is also the little child who leads, and the old sage or mentor, and Hermes, and the heroic leader, and the friendly animal. Each of these leads in a different way and to different conclusions. If her route and goal is not feeling, femininity, counter-sexuality, or eros – each of which did not stand the acid test in Part I – then what are we left with?

In chapter five we said anima is the archetype of psychic consciousness. But now we have been saying that anima is the archetype that mediates *un*consciousness. Putting these two statements together means that anima consciousness, consciousness of anima, means first of all awareness of one's unconsciousness. She brings the possibility of reflection in terms of the unconscious; i.e., in which way does this image, event, person, idea, feeling that is now the content of my reflection produce unconsciousness? This is the depth psychological viewpoint, and this is why anima (and not wise old man or mother nature or culture hero) is the archetype of the psychological calling. This is also why soul-making precedes self-individuating. For, before we can become conscious we must be able to know that we are unconscious, and where, when, and to what extent. Soul-making in this context becomes nothing more grandiose than the rather humiliating recognition of the anima archetype. It is first of all a "perception of differences" among her endless guiles and guises, seeing where we are entangled in her gossamers; it is an ongoing fantasy activity about fantasies. Here soul-making, to use an anima metaphor from Jung (CW 9,i, §158), refers to the "'discriminating knowledge'" that Prakrti evokes in Purusha by dancing before him. Purusha, by the way, does not use a sword for this discriminating. He watches.

Because anima mediates unconsciousness, making us not more conscious but less, she therefore flourishes where unconsciousness harbors: complexes, the illusion in life-attachments, states of drowsiness and mood, isolated reflection, hysterical wetness and vapors, and the follies of nympholepsy, those fascinations with natural, simple, innocent, and cloudy causes and cures and persons who embody them.

By believing that through integrating the manifestations we integrate and make conscious anima, we lose touch with the *autonomy* of her archetypal unconsciousness, and ours. The notion of unconsciousness means autonomous, spontaneous, ubiquitous,

137

(a) . . . the anima is always associated with the source of wisdom and enlightenment, whose symbol is the Old Wise Man. As long as you are under the influence of the anima you are unconscious of that archetype, i.e., you are identical with it and that explains your preoccupation with Indian philosophy. You are then forced to play the role of the Old Wise Man.

21 April 1948, Letter to Walter Lewino
(cf. on Sophia, pp. 39, 53 above)

(b) The symbolic process is an experience *in images and of images*.

CW 9, i, §82

(c) The numinosity of this archetype [the anima] causes a panic. . . . The reason for this lies in the fateful significance of the anima figure: she is the Sphinx of Oedipus, a Cassandra, the messenger of the Grail, the "white lady" who gives warning of death, etc.

. . . a man's consciousness projects all perceptions coming from the feminine personification of the unconscious onto an anima figure. . . . This explains the fateful quality of the anima. . . .

CW 10, §§713–14

Both these archetypes [the anima and animus] . . . possess a fatality that can on occasion produce tragic results. . . . It is only when we throw light into the dark depths of the psyche and explore the strange and tortuous paths of human fate that it gradually becomes clear to us how immense is the influence wielded by these two factors that complement our conscious life.   CW 9, ii, §41

. . . on a low level the anima is a caricature of the feminine Eros. . . . [T]he Eros of woman corresponds to *ming*, "fate" or "destiny". . . .   CW 13, §60

. . . the harbinger of fate, the anima. . . .   CW 13, §218

collective: it hits us ever and again, popping up and spilling out smack in the middle of the market place. Each event that occurs in a day has an entropic, disintegrating effect. Each conversation, analytical hour, meditation, and dream, by moving consciousness, makes us unconscious in a new way. She mediates these shifts in unconsciousness.

As consciousness of soul is primarily imaginal, that is, a self-reflection or recognition of the parade of fantasies which compose the psyche (chapter five above), she mediates the ceaseless movements of interiority. This interiority is not just within my head or within the proprioceptive gurgles of internal sensations. She reports the interiority of all attachments, whether in tandems to other persons (her gossip, suspicions, remembering resentments) or in the primordial tandems – spirit, body, and world – with which soul is attached and of which soul is the interiority.

But these reports are not answers. To ask the anima figure via active imagination for answers, to believe she brings counsel, other than the knowledge of not-knowing (ambiguity, indecision, uncertainty), is an analytical blunder no less foolish than those we explored earlier concerning her supposed eros or feeling or locus only in men. Jung suggests that her wisdom is actually an undifferentiated identification with the wise old man.[a] Even the knowledge that wise Sophia mediates is *pistis*, faith, a conviction in psychic reality and its fantasies, which leads one right away from knowing and toward imagining. The Gnostic world from where Sophia comes is a populated realm of imaginal figures, and the wisdom she mediates is participation in that realm.

Manifestations of the anima show that she has no answers: the images of her as innocent tell us of her ignorance, as echo tell us of her unoriginality, as slippery mermaid say that she is incomprehensible, just as her inability to speak clearly or think straight is imaged in the oracular sibyl and the muse.

The answers she does mediate are images.[b] She responds imaginatively and magically, stirring imagination to musings, inspirations, machinations, quests, and chases. These image-answers may have little to offer in a practical dilemma. Yet they touch fate: "Perhaps – who knows? – these eternal images are what men mean by fate" (CW 7, §183).[c] Perhaps, too, *amor fati*, the love of one's fate, is loving images. Images present themselves and in some way

can be known, but there always remains an unknowable, unfathomable depth to an image. Is this where fate resides? For fate is *the* unknown, in a way less known than death, which is an absolute surety. As anima pertains to unknowable fate, so all the deeper areas of her dominion are unknown: the archaic, phylogenetic past, the exotic cultures, the mystery religions of Goddesses, and the pre-conscious life of nature, as well as death. None of this can be known. To read her images and messages in dreams for pre-cognition is either a delusion or a hybris. Dream analysis brings us knowledge of dreams – not of life, of fate, or of death. Nor does dream analysis make the unconscious conscious; it merely moves illusions, offering a new opportunity for seeing through.

Anima consciousness clings to unconsciousness, as the nymphs adhere to their dense wooden trees and the echoes cannot leave their caves. It is an attached consciousness that sits like a small bird with a small voice upon the back of materia prima, roiling in the sludge of our stupidities, and so our possibility of greatest anima consciousness is where we are most unconsciously involved. Consequently, I have emphasized gossip, petty resentments, clinging needs, kitschy tastes, back-biting, old scores, and pouts. Not because these refer to inferior feelings of the anima or inferior femininity. Not at all. These conditions of intense attachment are thick with prima materia, offering the best ground for anima insights.

Anima consciousness not only relativizes ego consciousness but also relativizes the very idea of consciousness itself. It then is no longer clear when we are psychologically conscious and when unconscious. Even this fundamental discrimination, so important to the ego-complex, becomes ambiguous. Ego therefore tends to regard anima consciousness as elusive, capricious, vacillating. But these words describe a consciousness that is mediated to the unknown, conscious of its unconsciousness and, so, truly reflecting psychic reality.

Psychic reality, anima consciousness, soul-making – to be wrestling with any one of these involves us with the others. Soul-making calls for consciousness of anima, which is the archetype of

		I	II
(a)	1.	*Opus naturalium*	*Aqua*
	2.	*Divisio naturae*	*Terra*
	3.	*Anima*	*Aer*
	4.	*Intellectus*	*Ignis*

CW 9, ii, §414

soul and of psychic reality. But we can understand what is meant by "psychic reality" and "soul-making" no better than the anima allows us, and we can follow her no further than we can understand what is meant by the notion "anima," and by the notions "soul" and "psyche." In other words, just as a *psychological* intellect requires anima consciousness, anima consciousness requires psychological *intellect*. The soul would be understood. Psychological understanding thus consists of two interpenetrating constituents, psyche and logos, soul and intellect.

The interpenetration of intellectual understanding and soul occurs already in earlier notions of *psyché* in Greece and *anima* in Rome. As we have seen, these sometimes referred to a living generative air in the head, or soul in the breath, i.e., a psyche with logos, psychology. The "airs in the head" which Onians says refer to *anima* in the Latin tradition (chapter five, above) are a primary activity of the psyche, its production of "air-coloured" fantasies, the vaporous ephemera passing through the mind (pp. 25, 85, above, on air and anima).[a] The aerial phenomenology of the anima points not only to wispiness and flightiness. It also refers to one of the four primordial elements of the imagination (Bachelard). The alchemical psychologist Ripley said: "The aerial soul is the secret fire of our philosophy, our oil, our mystic water" (CW 12, §336n7). Air refers to the one invisible element, which like psychic reality we know only indirectly. If the aerial soul or airy anima is secret of the alchemical *opus* (and of course there are innumerable "secrets"), I would bring this psychic air into relation with *imaginatio*, "perhaps the most important key to the understanding of the *opus*" (ibid., §396). The secret and key to psychological work requires the airy imagination of the soul, that is, the capacity of imagining events "outside" (ibid.) of the natural bodily perspective of empirical and material literalism but in regard to a subtle or fantasy body of psychic reality. Being-in-soul requires being in a body too, but this body is built of soul stuff; it is a "breath-body" (CW 14, §748). Fantasy-images are this stuff, this "'subtle body'" (CW 12, §394).

So when we depreciate anima-airiness, or consider air insubstantial, we give lesser value to fantasy and to mind in general. Moreover and far worse, if that is possible, we lose the key to the entire psychological *opus*, the secret of which is body-building via

143

(a) They ["Syrena"] cause storms. . . .   CW 13, §218

(b) In psychotherapy it is a well-known fact that neurotic symptoms
     which seem impossible to attack can often be rendered harmless by
     conscious understanding. . . .   CW 13, §436 f.

     . . . aesthetic formulation needs understanding of the meaning, and
     understanding needs aesthetic formulation. The two supplement
     each other to form the transcendent function.   CW 8, §177

     . . . in the end it makes very little difference whether the doctor un-
     derstands or not, but it makes all the difference whether the pa-
     tient understands.   CW 16, §314

     . . . *lack of knowledge . . . has exactly the same effect as uncon-
     sciousness.*   CW 16, §546

(c) I am indeed convinced that creative imagination is the only pri-
     mordial phenomenon accessible to us, the real Ground of the psy-
     che, the only immediate reality. Therefore, I speak of *esse in ani-
     ma*, the only form of being we can experience directly.
                              10 January 1929, Letter to Kurt Plachte

     What indeed is reality if it is not a reality in ourselves, an *esse in
     anima*? Living reality is the product neither of the actual, objective
     behaviour of things nor of the formulated idea exclusively, but
     rather of the combination of both . . . through *esse in anima*.
                                                        CW 6, §77

(d) . . . the man's *opus* is concerned with the erotic aspect of the ani-
     ma. . . . Out of the *prima materia* grows the philosophical tree, the
     unfolding *opus*. . . . Eve [stands] for the man's anima who, as Sa-
     pientia or Sophia, produces out of her head the intellectual content
     of the work.   CW 16, §519

imagination. So we need to recollect the full range of psychic significance of the air element.

Anima-air pertains: to the tempests[a] named after her ("Anna," "Betty," "Carol" . . .) by the weather bureau; to the entire realm of internal weather, its pressure, its moisture, its mists; to enthusiasm and inspirations, explosions and collapses; to the creatures of the air like butterflies and spiders, angels and witches, little red balloons and gas-bags, every kind of bird and stinging winged thing; to distancing, depth of perspective and horizon, to invisibilities, and hunches that fall from the sky, auguries too; to the evocative power of scents, and to sound and song and speech, mind and intellect. The psychological intellect is itself an aspect of soul, one of its airy phenomena.

Jung's psychology derives from a thorough interpenetration of soul and intellect; that's why it understands, why it belongs among the psychologies of understanding (*verstehen*). Jung strongly urged the importance of understanding the psyche.[b] His understanding is based upon "*esse in anima*"[c] which provides the standpoint informing his psychological thinking and which makes his thought psychological. *Esse in anima* is also the basis of the massive body of his intellectual work.

Jung's *esse in anima* refers primarily to the "continually creative act" of fantasy (CW 6, §§77–78). But the term originates as a point of view within the universals arguments, a modus of soul between spirit and matter or between words and things. Now, we might call this point of view "psychological speculation," resulting from the speculum-mirror of anima reflection upon our spiritual and material involvements. By means of that mirror we engage in intellectual fantasy, build a psychology which can hold the psyche and which becomes its body. Out of head comes the opus, the material, embodied stuff of mind – and this too, as Jung says, is the work of Eve.[d]

(a) . . . the anima, personifies itself in a single figure.　　　CW 7, §332

Every man carries within him . . . a definite feminine image. . . . The same is true of the woman: she too has her inborn image of man. Actually, we know from experience that it would be more accurate to describe it as an image of *men*, whereas in the case of the man it is rather the image of *woman*.　　　CW 17, §338

. . . the "uni-personality" of the anima. . . . A passionate exclusiveness . . . attaches to the man's anima. . . .　　　CW 7, §338

(b) . . . as a rule, a woman's consciousness is restricted to one man, whereas a man's consciousness has a tendency to go beyond the one personal relationship. . . . In the unconscious, therefore, we may expect a compensation by contraries. The man's sharply defined anima figure fulfils this expectation perfectly, as also does the indefinite polymorphism of the woman's animus.　　　CW 10, §81

With regard to the plurality of the animus as distinguished from what we might call the "uni-personality" of the anima, this remarkable fact seems to me to be a correlate of the conscious attitude.　　　CW 7, §338

(c) As it is made up of a plurality of preconceived opinions, the animus is far less susceptible of personification by a single figure, but appears more often as a group or crowd. . . . On a low level the animus is an inferior Logos, . . . just as on a low level the anima is a caricature of the feminine Eros. . . . Eros is relatedness, Logos is discrimination. . . .　　　CW 13, §60

(d) . . . sex is determined by a majority of male or female genes. . . . But the minority of genes belonging to the other sex does not simply disappear. A man therefore has in him a feminine side. . . . I have called this figure the "anima". . . .　　　CW 9, i, §512

9. *Anima as Uni-Personality*

A SUBSIDIARY definition of the anima is that there is only one image of her in a man's psyche,[a] whereas the animus is defined as a multiplicity (CW 10, §81 – "he is not so much a unity as a plurality"). "The woman's incubus consists of a host of masculine demons; the man's succubus is a vampire" (CW 7, §370).

Jung accounts for this difference between anima and animus mainly through social and historical differences in gender roles: women are more individually related and monogamous in consciousness, men more indiscriminately related and polygamous; these attitudes find compensation in unconscious contrasexual positions.[b] But the account may also be put as a Jungian contrast between the differentiation of spirits (animus) and the unifying power of eros (anima).[c] Another account (that I have not found in Jung) elaborates a biological analogy similar to one that Jung does use,[d] that of male and female genes. Sperm are many, the ovum one; so, animus is a multiplicity, anima a unity.[43]

(a) *The dreamer is surrounded by a throng of vague female forms....*
The figures that appear in the dream are ... pointing to the
feminine nature of the unconscious. They are fairies or fascinating
sirens and lamias ... who infatuate the lonely wanderer and lead
him astray.   CW 12, §§58–61

(b) ... primitives assume the existence of several souls.... I am therefore inclined to think that autonomous complexes are among the
normal phenomena of life and that they make up the structure of
the unconscious psyche.   CW 8, §§217–18

... it is frequently supposed that people have two or more
souls....   CW 8, §577

The plurality of souls indicates a plurality of relatively autonomous complexes....   CW 8, §587

(c) This is an age-old experience of mankind which is reflected in the
universal supposition of a plurality of souls in one and the same individual. As the plurality of psychic components at the primitive
level shows, the original state is one in which the psychic processes
are very loosely knit and by no means form a self-contained unity.
                                                        CW 8, §365

It strikes me as significant, particularly in regard to our hypothesis
of a multiple consciousness and its phenomena, that the characteristic alchemical vision of sparks scintillating in the blackness of the
arcane substance should, for Paracelsus, change into the spectacle
of the "interior firmament" and its stars....
... it is in my view not too much to assume that these multiple
luminosities correspond to tiny conscious phenomena.
                                                        CW 8, §§392–96

Now I do not want to question the phenomenological findings either of Jung (including CW 12, §§58–61 where anima appears significantly as a multiplicity[a]) or of later analytical psychologists in regard to the unity or plurality of the anima. (To repeat: this essay is written not within an empirical fantasy but within a critical one. We are thinking about thoughts, not about things, or about the effect of thoughts upon our experience of things.) But we do have to explore the *notion* of unity and multiplicity since it enters into the anima's definition.

The main question opened by these pairings is the ancient and perplexing issue concerning the unity or multiplicity of soul. Jung points to the multiplicity of souls in several contexts. "The primitive assertion that the individual has a plurality of souls is in agreement with our findings" (CW 14, §504n386).[b] By "primitive" Jung means "primordial" (CW 8, §218) and therefore always present at our deepest levels, since a multiplicity of autonomous complexes "make up the structure of the unconscious psyche" (ibid.).[c]

(a) I have always been greatly impressed by the character of dissociated fragments as personalities.... [I]f such fragments have personality, the whole from which they were broken off must have personality to an even higher degree.... *Personality need not imply consciousness. It can just as easily be dormant or dreaming.*

    ... It may be that all of the [hidden] personality to be found in the unconscious is contained in the fragmentary personifications mentioned before....

    ... in the unconscious of every man there is hidden a feminine personality.... CW 9, i, §§508–11

(b) The classical world thought of this pneuma as Dionysus . . . whose divine substance is distributed throughout the whole of nature.

CW 11, §387

Psychologically, this doctrine testifies to the personality- or ego-character of psychic complexes: just as the distinguishing mark of the ego-complex is consciousness, so it is possible that other, "unconscious" complexes may possess, as splinter psyches, a certain luminosity of their own. CW 14, §47

    ... the motif of dismemberment . . . is well known in alchemy. The atoms are or become "white sparks" shining in the *terra foetida.* CW 14, §64

In actual fact, however, the psychic substratum, that dark realm of the unknown, exercises a fascinating attraction that threatens to become the more overpowering the further he penetrates into it. [fn.48: Symbolized by a sorceress or by wanton girls . . .] The psychological danger that arises here is the disintegration of personality into its functional components, i.e., the separate functions of consciousness, the complexes, hereditary units, etc....

    ... that is to say, the body and the psychic representatives of the organs gain mastery over the conscious mind.

CW 12, §§439–40

Another excursion on psychic multiplicity leads directly into a review of the anima concept.[a] We find multiplicity again in his idea of soul fragments dispersed throughout matter and body,[b] a subject that I went into via "Dionysus in Jung's Writings" (*Spring 1972*; reprinted in *Facing the Gods*). At times Jung seems to agree with the description of the self as the "collective aggregate of all individual souls" and to be "compounded of many," quoting Origen: "Each of us is not one, but many" (CW 9,i, §675).

The history of psychology shows many kinds or parts of soul, or soul-systems with specific names – animal, corporal, sanguinal, rational, seminal, spiritual, mercurial, vegetative, sensitive, vital – and has located these souls in different zones and regions of the actual human and animal being. Alchemy is replete with these names of soul as is pre-modern medicine. As well, multiplicity of souls is commonly found by anthropologists investigating the psychological conceptions of pre-literate peoples. These different kinds of soul express the idea that there is a psychic aspect, or animation, within or attached to every bit of physical nature, an "organ consciousness" (CW 15, §112n8).

And myths love to enchant us with the figures of innumerable maidens, such as the Gopi girls of Krishna, the Houris of Persian paradise, or the multiple daughters of the Sun who show Parmenides the way to truth. A delight in multiplicity and multiple delights seem to belong to anima phenomenology.

(a) On the one hand the anima is the connecting link with the world beyond and the eternal images, while on the other hand her emotionality involves man in the chthonic world and its transitoriness.

CW 13, §457

... the anima, as she personifies the plurality of the archetypes ...

CW 14, §218

(b) [The anima] ... in accordance with her Eros nature, wears the features of Aphrodite, Helen (Selene), Persephone, and Hecate.

CW 9, ii, §41

(c) His [Prometheus's] soul is Minerva.... The Prometheus of mythology has his soul-relation with Pandora or Athene....

CW 6, §§289–95

(d) ... the Kore as observable in man, the *anima*.   CW 9, i, §356

(e) ... Pandora has the value of a soul-image....   CW 6, §305

(f) Four stages of eroticism were known in the late classical period: Hawwah (Eve), Helen (of Troy), the Virgin Mary, and Sophia.... [W]e are dealing with the ... anima-figure in four stages....

CW 16, §361

... the four female figures of the Gnostic underworld, Eve, Helen, Mary, and Sophia.   CW 15, §211

Unlike philosophy, and scientific medicine too, which chooses among statements, aiming always toward a coherent unity, or unified field, psychology may include all the positions about soul as valid descriptions. Each statement reflects a valid reality; each is an expression of soul telling about itself according to its present constellation. Because anima comprises so many contrarieties, a psychology true to anima describes soul in so many contrary ways. From the perspective of delight in plurality, anima as a uni-personality is merely one of her many guises.

Anima specifically connects with plurality through its definition as representative of the collective unconscious involving us in innumerable images and body-bound emotions.[a] Anima and plurality again connect in the idea that the "anima/animus stage is correlated with polytheism, the self with monotheism" (CW 9, ii, §427), a statement that opened a considerable discussion in *Spring 1971*, pp. 193–232.

Because anima is "the matrix of all the divine and semi-divine figures, from the pagan goddess to the Virgin" (CW 16, §504), her images range through a variety of figures from Gnosticism and classical polytheism. Jung mentions Aphrodite, Selene, Persephone, Hecate,[b] Athene-Minerva,[c] Kore,[d] and Pandora[e] besides the four classical "stages" of the anima[f] and the elf, nixie, and nymph creatures we have already referred to. He also draws parallels with the doubling of souls in Egyptian, Hebrew, and Chinese thought. Clearly, when describing the anima, Jung's imagination turns frequently to the polyvalence of pagan myth and to primitive or exotic ideas of soul, i.e., to reflections that are extra- or pre-Christian.

(a) *The dreamer is surrounded by a throng of vague female forms....*
The figures that appear in the dream are . . . pointing to the feminine nature of the unconscious. They are fairies or fascinating sirens and lamias, . . . who infatuate the lonely wanderer and lead
him astray.   CW 12, §§58–61

(b) The splitting of the anima into many figures is equivalent to dissolution into an indefinite state, i.e., into the unconscious, from
which we may conjecture that a relative dissolution of the conscious mind is running parallel with the historical regression (a
process to be observed in its extreme form in schizophrenia).
                                                        CW 12, §116

Despite these passages, the definition of anima as a "'uni-personality'" (CW 7, §338) means that when the anima appears in plural form[a] a regressive "dissolution"[b] must be taking place. Moreover, each man has one anima figure that truly represents his soul. Even if the psyche is a plurality of complexes, each with its soul-spark, *one man, one anima* is the formula.

The first advantage of anima unity is practical. It limits. It places a stricture upon our use of the term. We may not call "anima" every female figure, mood, and aesthetic or historical concern. Without this stricture every cat-like creature, every waitress, telephone operator, usherette becomes anima, as well as sisters, nieces, daughters, cousins, and so on through the public, familial, historical, literary, legendary worlds. Then, as Graham Hough already recognized (*Spring 1973*, p. 93):

> . . . we are faced with an *embarras de richesse*: . . . Are all the heroines of romantic and idealised fiction anima figures? Yes. Are they equally anima figures regardless of the quality of the fictions in which they appear? I am afraid, yes. . . . From Dante's Beatrice and Petrarch's Laura to the vulgarest heroines of soap-operas and girlie magazines, all are recognisable as anima images.

The notion of only one empirical anima configuration says no to this sloppiness. We may call "anima" only that particular gestalt which precisely, continually, and specifically signifies the core quality of my soul. This gestalt must also bear definitive attributes that are archetypally anima: mystery, emotion, paradox, importance; she must stir my loving and link backwards through tradition to pre-history, trailing the archaic, phylogenetic and psychotic psyche in her roots; as well, she must be instrumental to fate and be the prime mover of fantasy and reflection by remaining "unknown."

To be replete with all these attributes is a tall order for any one figure to fill. What about all the figures that fill only some aspects – do we drop the epithet "anima" from them or accord it nonetheless though in diminished strength? In other words we have been forced back to the same problem: one anima or many. Before we try to work on this in another way, let's look at the effects in therapy of the uni-personality notion.

(a) ... start some dialogue with your anima.... put a question or two to her: why she appears as Beatrice? why she is so big? why you are so small? why she nurses your wife and not yourself? ... Treat her as a person, if you like as a patient or a goddess, but above all treat her as something that does exist.... talk to this person ... to see what she is about and to learn what her thoughts and character are. If you yourself step into your fantasy, then that overabundance of material will soon come to more reasonable proportions.... Keep your head and your own personality over against the overwhelming multitude of images.... treat the anima as if she were a patient whose secret you ought to get at.

7 May 1947, Letter to Mr. O.

[The patient] ... is quite right to treat the anima as an autonomous personality and to address personal questions to her.

I mean this as an actual technique.... The art of it consists only in allowing our invisible partner to make herself heard.... [O]ne should cultivate the art of conversing with oneself in the setting provided by an affect....   CW 7, §§322–23

(b) ... scintilla, the "little soul-spark" of Meister Eckhart.... Similarly Heraclitus ... is said to have conceived the soul as a "spark of stellar essence."...

Alchemy, too, has its doctrine of the scintilla.... "For all things have their origin in this source...."   CW 14, §§42–43

Were it not for the leaping and twinkling of the soul, man would rot away in his greatest passion, idleness.   CW 9, i, §56

The therapeutic recommendation to concentrate upon the anima through dialogue with her[a] knits her into a more centered and defined figure. When my therapeutic intention accords with the notion of uni-personality, I will be aiming for a single figure who can be my muse or genie, draining off affects from subsidiary fantasies, forsaking all others, by definition.

Definitions are rules that have all the power of ruling principles, determining what belongs and what is excluded. If multiplicity and anima become by definition mutually exclusive, then not only is my individual soul-image deprived of unlimited multiplicity, but also *multiplicity is deprived of soul* – and indeed in much of Jung's writings on Dionysus, multiplicity is a threat to soul. In other places (e.g., CW 9, i, §279), where he contrasts unity and plurality, the latter refers to "dissociation," "fragmentation," "dissolution," or at best an "incomplete synthesis of personality."

Deep under the surface of therapy's skirmishes with anima unification, there rumble great battle chariots of antiquity, persecutions, and the slaughter of martyrs. For within our engagement with anima lies *the* historical conflict in the Western soul about the soul. Is it "Christian" or "Classical" (or "Pagan" as the Christians called Classical culture)? Anima as uni-personality takes her stand within the main line of the Christian view of soul.[44] Then the pagan elements excluded from anima lose soul and become demonized areas of guilt and inferiority. They are only soul-sparks,[b] splinters, splits, but never are they fully able to become soul unless their energy is transformed and held by the dominant anima system of Mistress Soul as Mother Church.[45] Unification through transformation is an equivalent in psychological language to what religion calls conversion of soul.

But what of the soul-sparks, the anima fragments that do not cohere, do not convert? These always threaten a great conflagra-

(a) Only a little more than a thousand years ago we stumbled out of the crudest beginnings of polytheism into a highly developed Oriental religion which lifted the imaginative minds of half-savages to a height that in no way corresponded to their spiritual development.... The repressed elements naturally did not develop, but went on vegetating in the unconscious, in their original barbarism. CW 13, §70

Spiritually the Western world is in a precarious situation, and the danger is greater the more we blind ourselves ... with illusions about our beauty of soul. Western man lives in a thick cloud of incense which he burns to himself so that his own countenance may be veiled from him in the smoke.
  ... that megalomania of ours which leads us to suppose ... that Christianity is the only truth and the white Christ the only redeemer.
  No wonder that unearthing the psyche is like undertaking a full-scale drainage operation. CW 10, §§183–86

Christian civilization has proved hollow to a terrifying degree: it is all veneer, but the inner man has remained untouched and therefore unchanged.... Inside reign the archaic gods, supreme as of old.... CW 12, §12

(b) The Christian principle which unites the opposites is the *worship of God,* in Buddhism it is the *worship of the self* (self-development), while in Spitteler and Goethe it is the *worship of the soul* symbolized by the *worship of woman.* Implicit in this categorization is the modern individualistic principle on the one hand, and on the other a primitive poly-daemonism which assigns to every race, every tribe, every family, every individual its specific religious principle. CW 6, §375

(c) The animus does not appear as one person, but as a plurality of persons. CW 7, §332 (cf. CW 10, §698)

  ... the woman's animus ... his name is legion. CW 9, ii, §424

tion. They are the pre-Christian level always at the threshold, a recurring fantasy in Jung's writings[a] – "how thin is the wall that separates us from pagan times" (CW 9, ii, §272). In fact Jung explicitly connects – in a remarkable paragraph on "the worship of woman and the worship of the soul" in the Romantics[b] – "the modern individualistic principle" and "primitive poly-daemonism." In this fantasy of soul, Christian and Pagan constellate and compensate each other. The fantasy of barbarian hinterlands, Wotan, Dionysus, and the "poly-daemonic" unconscious that has not been Christianized – all contrast strongly with the fantasy of the individualized "uni-personality" of soul who is the guide of individuation toward unified wholeness. Anima is thus *anima naturaliter christiana*, the soul as naturally Christian because of her uni-personality definition. But! – should the contrast between the one and the many be placed within the model of compensation, then the more the soul image coalesces into unity, is not the likelihood increased at the same time of even more psychotic and barbaric threats behind the thin wall? In other words: the anxiety of some analysts about latent psychosis in their patients may be a direct consequent of their anima notion. Worship of the unified anima and "primitive poly-daemonism" are two sides of the same coin.

To say it another way: a unified, unconscious anima constellates its opposite, polygamous consciousness, in the masculine ego. The multiple, unconscious animus constellates its opposite, monogamous consciousness, in the feminine ego. Archetypally, what is going on is projection in a reverse direction. Then we see monogamy to be an idea born of the animus: an attempt to discriminate among the many spirits by choosing one and sticking by it.[c] And polygamy is an idea born of anima, an attempt to loosen masculine, compulsive singleness by paganizing and demonizing with multiplicity.

By evoking the Christian–Pagan conflict, I am trying to make explicit the historical background in Jung's fantasy regarding this question. I am trying to grasp why he had to insist on unity of anima in face of evidence that could just as well have turned it the other way. But evidence is not the determining factor, neither in our discussion nor probably in Jung's notion. There is something deeper at work, the subjective factor, which partly forms the empirical ground of every anima definition.

(a) ... I caught sight of two figures, an old man with a white beard and a beautiful young girl.... The old man explained that he was Elijah, and that gave me a shock. But the girl staggered me even more, for she called herself Salome! She was blind. What a strange couple: Salome and Elijah. But Elijah assured me that he and Salome had belonged together from all eternity.   MDR, p. 181

(b) It has been objected that Christ cannot have been a valid symbol of the self.... I can agree with this view only if it refers strictly to the present time, when psychological criticism has become possible, but not if it pretends to judge the pre-psychological age. Christ did not merely *symbolize* wholeness, but, as a psychic phenomenon, he *was* wholeness.   CW 9, ii, §115n75

The Christ-symbol is of the greatest importance for psychology in so far as it is perhaps the most highly developed and differentiated symbol of the self, apart from the figure of the Buddha. We can see this from the scope and substance of all the pronouncements that have been made about Christ: they agree with the psychological phenomenology of the self in unusually high degree, although they do not include all aspects of this archetype.   CW 12, §22

(c) ... hysteria is characterized by a centrifugal movement of libido....   CW 6, §859 (cf. §§858–63)

(d) She [Eve, Pandora] played the part ... of the anima, who functions as the link between body and spirit, just as Shakti or Maya entangles man's consciousness with the world.   CW 13, §126

(e) ... in schizophrenia the movement is more centripetal.... During the incubation of his illness the schizophrenic ... turns away from the outer world in order to withdraw into himself....
     CW 6, §§859–63

Therefore I do not believe that the question can be resolved merely philosophically, i.e., that anima as a noumenal archetype is one; anima as phenomenal images is many. This kind of out leaves the door open for new questions to crowd in. The leading one is: how do we know that the noumenal anima is 'one' since the noumenal is beyond knowledge? All we know are the many anima images, and they appear the world over as Hough points out, and they appear in particular in each person's variegated imagination. Answers such as the-many-in-the-one and the-one-in-the-many are conundrums or wise saws: the psychology of the matter is still untouched.

Rather I believe the question is resolvable only in terms of another anima tandem. This time it is the tandem which has highest place in Jung's psychology – the soul/self pair or anima/wise old man. They appeared early in Jung's imagination as Salome with Elijah-Philemon.[a] With them comes an "Egypto-Hellenistic atmosphere with a Gnostic coloration," the very world rife with conflict between Christian and Classical for the soul of Western man. It is within a tandem to wise old man (senex) that anima is perceived and defined as a uni-personality, not because she *is* one but because she is *seen* through an eye that sees 'ones.' The point of view is from the self archetype which sees soul with a unified eye.[46] ". . . if therefore thine eye be single, thy whole body shall be full of light" (Matt. 6:22). The unipersonal anima finds its background in tandem with self, its centricity and unity, its transcending synthesis and inwardness – and its Christianity. For it is less the soul that is naturally Christian than it is the *self* that has naturally been symbolized in our culture by Christ.[b]

Here the notion of anima is affected by another group of oppositional pairings. On the one hand: outside, centrifugal extraversion, hysteria,[c] "multiplicity of the world" (CW 9,i, §632), and anima in the wrong place creating all the illusions of Shakti.[d] On the other: inside, centripetal introversion, schizophrenia,[e] the ar-

(a) The withdrawal of projections makes the anima what she originally was: an archetypal image which, in its right place, functions to
the advantage of the individual. CW 16, §504

Melusina, the deceptive Shakti. . . . should no longer dance before
the adept with alluring gestures, but must become what she was
from the beginning: a part of his wholeness. As such she must be
"conceived in the mind." CW 13, §223

(b) In the shape of the goddess the anima is manifestly projected, but
in her proper (psychological) shape she is *introjected*; she is, as
Layard says, the "anima within." She is the natural *sponsa*, man's
mother or sister or daughter or wife from the beginning, the companion whom the endogamous tendency vainly seeks to win in the
form of mother and sister. CW 16, §438

chaic, primordial imagination of myth and anima in the "right place."[a] The extraverted movement is Epimethean, "constantly giving out and responding in a soulless fashion" (CW 6, §310), whereas the introverted movement presents anima functioning appropriately, endogamous, "within,"[b] mediatrix to archetypal images (not patterns of behavior). Anima development thus proceeds from outside to inside as well as from lower to higher (Eve to Sophia), quite in accordance with St. Augustine's prescription for the soul's development: *"ab exterioribus ad interiore, ab inferioribus ad superioria."*

By mediating to the center and its unity rather than to the periphery and its soulless ten thousand things, the uni-personality notion implies three fundamental movements for anima development: from many to one, from outer to inner, from lower to higher. When these notions are taken literally as ways to behave, then anima 'development' actually results in a superiority, an anima inflation, and then too unification is brought about at the expense of the lower, outer, and multiple events of the soul. Anima has indeed led to wise old man, but as a dogmatic, literal-encrusted senex.

The consequences of this movement – if not thoroughly larded with the richness of Jung's thought about psychic plurality and the myriad possibilities of soul figures, soul emotions, and soul sparks – may shrivel consciousness to the one-sidedness that Jung considered a definition of neurosis. I would specify the neurosis as *religious* and find its etiology in analysis itself, because it would be fostered by the analytical notions of anima. Moreover, this neurosis would go unnoticed in the consulting room since the attitudes of the patient would comply with the anima fantasy of the therapy.

By the religious neurosis of analysis, I mean specifically what happens when individuation is guided by a notion of anima that takes integration as unity and interiority as superiority. Then one finds soul only by turning inward to a single guide. By concentrating upon this uni-personality, she herself becomes concentrated, drawing off the surplus exuberance of fantasy. When this concentration of anima dominates, it exudes the sanctimonious balm of superiority that seeps through the analysis as a by-product of its identification with interiority. Then anima loses her ties with life of which she is the very archetype. A peculiar religiosity, together

(a) The plurality of Ufos ... is a projection of a number of psychic images of wholeness which appear in the sky because on the one hand they represent archetypes charged with energy and on the other hand are not recognized as psychic factors.

CW 10, §635 (cf. §§633–34)

(b) The goal [unity] is important only as an idea; the essential thing is the *opus* which leads to the goal: *that* is the goal of a lifetime.

CW 16, §400

Personality, as the complete realization of our whole being, is an unattainable ideal. But unattainability is no argument against the ideal, for ideals are only signposts, never the goal.

CW 17, §291

with the soul-magic of synchronicity, anoints the analysis, and the worldly failures, obtuseness, and insignificance of the two persons become mere wrappings within which are hid higher powers of wisdom regarding the 'inner' world, analysis its glass vessel. Then, *horribile dictu*, individuation becomes insulation, introversion becomes introspection, and insights are replaced by inspirations, as soul merges with the spirituality of a logos Self, so that the enigmas of life are resolved *in vitro* by means of internal dialogues with an oracular priestess, 'my anima.'

"But the striving for unity is opposed by a possibly even stronger tendency to create multiplicity, so that even in strictly monotheistic religions like Christianity the polytheistic tendency cannot be suppressed" (CW 5, §149). The irrepressible many return from the far periphery as multiple flying saucers, a plurality of units.[a] A similar plurality of units occurs at the culminating stage of the alchemical work "beyond which it is impossible to go except by means of the *multiplicatio*" (CW 16, §526). For unity, Jung reminds us, is not an empirical reality, not part of our lived world. It is the fantasy image of a goal.[b] "Reality consists of a multiplicity of things. But one is not a number; the first number is two, and with it multiplicity and reality begin" (CW 14, §659). "So far, I have found no stable or definite center in the unconscious and I don't believe such a center exists. I believe that the thing which I call the Self is an ideal center...."[47]

Jung's insistence upon the paradoxical nature of the Self becomes especially important in regard to its definition as archetype of psychic unity. Because by definition it is always partly unconscious, it has no closure and is therefore susceptible to interfusion with other archetypal dominants. The notion of Self and even an experience or dream image called Self will be subject to the coloring of other archetypes. So, there are notions and experiences that impress shadow on Self (darkness, unknowing, the *sol niger*), or great mother (cyclical in time or regenerative in effect), or anima (natural, aesthetic, and historical symbols). Self is not self-same, and as a "stable and definite center" it is an ideal. Ideals lead to idealizations, so that a therapeutic focus on Self is better conceived

(a) The anima/animus stage is correlated with polytheism. . . .

CW 9, ii, §427

The transformation of libido through the symbol is a process that has been going on ever since the beginnings of humanity and continues still. . . . This age-old function of the symbol is still present today, despite the fact that for many centuries the trend of mental development has been towards the suppression of individual symbol-formation. . . . [A] step[s] in this direction was . . . the extermination of polytheism. . . .   CW 8, §92

if it attends to its differentiations – that is, the actual language, image, and feelings – in order to recognize under which dominant, within which myth, Self is now appearing.

Just as the within is not literally inside me and the superior not literally higher, so unity is not literally singleness, in one place, one voice, one image. Just as the within refers to the point of view of interiority everywhere and the higher refers to the subtle fantasy aspect of events, so unity of anima refers to the recognition that all things are ways of soul and signify it, that existence is a psychic network, and that nothing given to human being is alien to soul. Unity of soul refers to unity of an outlook that sees all events as psychic realities. A uni-personality of anima personifies this unified perspective. By means of it we recognize that the ten thousand attachments represented by the multiplicity of anima images and experiences are each and all soul-making possibilities. Anima is the function that gives psyche to multiplicity by being the psychological correlate to polytheism and to individual symbol formations.[a] Anima enables the many not to become one but to become psychic *materia*. Then anima cannot have any specific known identity, cannot be identified. "Anima" refers to the viewpoint of soul that we bring (or she brings) toward experience. Then the question of one or many is psychologically irrelevant and, as Jung himself says, the anima can be "in singular or plural form" (CW 14, §128).

10. The Anima in the Syzygy

SO FAR we have generally been examining the anima notion independent of its context within the field of archetypes. Even if this aids conceptual clarification, it can result in phenomenological distortion since the archetypes by definition are inextricably inter-

(a) Together they [anima and animus] form a divine pair.... the divine syzygy....   CW 9, ii, §41 (cf. §§25–42)

twined "in a state of contamination, of the most complete mutual interpenetration and interfusion."[48]

> The discriminating intellect naturally keeps on trying to establish their singleness of meaning and thus misses the essential point; for what we can above all establish as the one thing consistent with their nature is their *manifold meaning*, their almost limitless wealth of reference, which makes any unilateral formulation impossible. (CW 9,i, §80)

The archetypal field presents a polycentric picture, a theater of personified powers always implicating one another. The perspective that would cleanly etch out their distinct lines reflects the monotheistic consciousness of the scientific and philosophical approach; the perspective that would speak of them ambiguously and in images reflects the polytheistic, hermetic, or anima consciousness of the psychological approach.

From this second position every archetype always implies another: child—mother, mother—hero, hero—father, father—son, son—wise old man, wise old man—daughter, daughter—mother, mother—child – and so on, no matter where we start or how we proceed. Alchemy excels in exemplifying this interlocking of terms, where each term shifts its valence according to the constellation. Thus anima can have all sorts of names and valences and images depending upon the tandem she is in. We seem able to grasp her essence only in contradistinction to something else. Usually this contradistinction has been identified with contrasexuality. But we have also reported upon anima in tandems with ego, shadow, persona, and self.

But of all the tandems and couplings, it is especially with the animus that this notion is paired. Jung calls this pair the syzygy.[a] He says: "Anyone, therefore, who does not know the . . . significance of the *syzygy* motif . . . can hardly claim to say anything about the concept of the anima" (CW 9,i, §115). His last major treatments of anima in 1951 (CW 9,ii, §20 ff.), 1954 (CW 9,i, §111 ff.), and 1955–56 (CW §14) consider anima and animus together. They are exemplifications in psychological experience of the archetypal image of the divine conjuncted pair, the syzygy.

Now we can look back at all the contrasted pairings (e.g., multi- and uni-personality in chapter nine, anima- and ego-consciousness

... the syzygy motif ... expresses the fact that a masculine element is always paired with a feminine one.   CW 9, i, §134

in chapter five, contra-sexuality in chapter one) as ineluctable consequences, even literalizations, of the syzygy. Now we can see why our enquiry has been shadowed from the beginning by a style of viewing anima through an opposite. The archetypal perspective of the syzygy will always perceive events in compensatory pairings.

This must be so, for in "the realm of the syzygies" "the One is never separated from the Other" (CW 9, i, §194). If anima belongs archetypally to this pair, we "can hardly lay claim to say anything about the concept of anima" without speaking also of animus. Phenomenally she can never appear alone without him.[a] *To be engaged with anima is to be engaged simultaneously with animus in some way or another.*

The implications of this are staggering, so let us move cautiously. Have all our scrutinizings and speculations been vain since we have not fully taken into account the other half of the archetypal pair? Or, has the Other been present throughout in the perspectives toward the anima, and thus in the author, making this essay on anima both an *esse in anima* and an animus exercise? For if anima has been the subject of investigation, animus has been the investigator. Or does it work the other way around—if animus has been the logos plan and the activity of making words serve critical discrimination, anima has been feathering those words and guiding their direction with her fantasies. We cannot take any stand regarding anima without, *horribile dictu*, taking up an animus position. There is no *other* vantage point toward either than the other. And since the syzygy insists that we cannot have one without the other, we cannot intuit or fantasy our way beyond the archetypal limitations placed on all consciousness of either member of this pair by the pair itself. "From this fact we may reasonably conclude that man's imagination is bound by this [syzygy] motif, so that he was largely compelled to project it again and again, at all times and in all places" (CW 9, i, §120).

This essay is one more of those compelled projections, part of the endless mythologizing about divine pairs, stimulated by them and reflecting them: Aphrodite *peitho* (persuasion), persuasive rhetoric joined alternatively with Hephaistos in the forging of constructions and with Ares in battle rage. This essay is a mythical activity of anima coming on as a critical activity of animus. Yet just this is psychology, the interpenetration of psyche and logos, within

(a) ... the motif of *polyophthalmia* ... point[s] to the peculiar nature of the unconscious, which can be regarded as a "multiple consciousness."

CW 9,i, §614

(b) ... the soul (*anima*) released at the "death" is reunited with the dead body and brings about its resurrection, or again the "many colours" ... or "peacock's tail" ... lead to the one white colour that contains all colours.

CW 12, §334

(c) ... the archetypes appear as active personalities in dreams and fantasies.

CW 9,i, §80

the bounds of the syzygy who sets the limits to our psychological field so that we cannot imagine beyond it. *Within* it, however, our possibilities are as limitless as the ceaseless pairings and couplings and interpenetrations of anima and animus.

To imagine in pairs and couples is to think mythologically. Mythical thinking connects pairs into tandems rather than separating them into opposites which is anyway a mode of philosophy. Opposites lend themselves to very few kinds of description: contradictories, contraries, complementaries, negations – formal and logical. Tandems, however, like brothers or enemies or traders or lovers show endless varieties of styles. Tandems favor intercourse – innumerable positions. Opposition is merely one of the many modes of being in a tandem.

The notion of the syzygy demands that an exhaustive exploration of anima examine animus to the same extent. To do her full justice one has to give him equal time. But this has been happening indirectly. All our observations have come from a contrasting position, and each of these other positions can be conceived as representing the other, the animus, in one of his perspectives. This gives some justification to an old argument of Neumann's (chapter four) that the development of ego consciousness in men and women alike was essentially a masculine process (or protest) out of a feminine unconscious. There is the syzygy once more. They play into each other, constellated by particular patterns, or mythologems. Some we have already seen: chapter nine, where the unity–plurality controversy turns anima into a polyopthalmic,[a] multicolored peacock's tail[b] and animus into a monotheistic cyclops; chapter seven, where one notion of integrating the anima conceives her as a dark dragon and him as a loin-girded swords-man.

By continuing to call the syzygy "her" and "him," I am stressing their personified nature.[c] Persons come in genders, even if psychic persons do indeed transgress this naturalism (as Rupprecht's Martial Maid shows in *Spring 1974*, pp. 269–93). Jung notes that: "The male-female syzygy is only one among the possible pairs of opposites" (CW 9,i, §142). He hints in the same paragraph that in itself anima and animus may have no special sexual gender, or as I tried to put it above (p. 65): "Paradoxically, the very archetype of femininity may not itself be feminine."

(a)

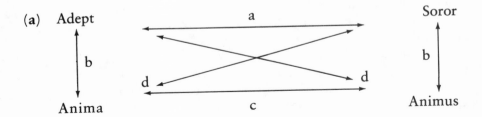

. . . .

(a) An uncomplicated personal relationship.

(b) A relationship of the man to his anima and of the woman to her animus.

(c) A relationship of anima to animus and *vice versa*.

(d) A relationship of the woman's animus to the man (which happens when the woman is identical with her animus), and of the man's anima to the woman (which happens when the man is identical with his anima).

CW 16, §§422–23 (cf. CW 9, ii, §§328, 359–98;

CW 14, §§611–12; CW 16, §§431–32)

(b) On the psychological level, the tangle of relationships in the cross-cousin marriage reappears in the transference problem. The dilemma here consists in the fact that anima and animus are projected upon their human counterparts. . . . But in so far as anima and animus undoubtedly represent the contrasexual components of the personality, their kinship character . . . point[s] . . . to the integration of personality. . . .   CW 16, §441

Nonetheless, essential to thinking in syzygies is thinking in genders. Unfortunately, the next step in analytical psychology has been identifying these genders with actual men and women, coupling kinds of syzygies between man-and-anima, woman-and-animus, man-and-woman, and fourth, anima-and-animus, even with diagrams, for example, the lengthy discussion of the Gnostic symbol of the Self.[a]

Anima–animus, the fourth of these syzygies, has two meanings: a) a syzygy between two persons in an interpersonal relation, and b) a syzygy of anima and animus *within* any man or any woman as an *intrapersonal* relation. It is this latter that needs real attention. It has been neglected because we have been locked into the contrasexual definition of anima and animus. But, as we worked out above (pp. 51–65), archetypes cannot be confined to human gender, and we saw how anima works equally in women. The next consequent is to observe animus working in men.

The archetypal syzygy takes place inside us each and not only as projected into our relationships.[b] That's why men carry on and talk like animuses, and women gaze and fade like animas. To account for this everyday behavior in terms of "animus of the mother" or "anima of the animus," etc. – contortions that analysts have had to resort to – misses a main point about anima–animus projections.

Projections occur between parts of the psyche, not only outside into the world. They occur between internal persons and not only onto external people. The alchemical idea of projection referred to *interior* events. Ruland's alchemical dictionary describes projection as a "violent interpenetration" of substances; there is a "sudden egression" which is projected over a matter by another matter therewith transforming it. Projection too can be psychologized; we can take back projection itself, interiorizing it as an activity going on blindly between anima and animus within.

Each anima figure projects a particular sort of animus figure and vice versa.[49] A Hebe wants a Hercules and Hercules does it for Hebe – and not just on the college campus between cheerleader and linebacker but "in here." My hebephrenic soul, young and silly and tied by social conventions, the bride and her shower, produces an ego that comes home like a hero showing off and bearing tro-

phies. Or, within the smiling, innocent girl is ruthless ambition in a lionskin, forever wrestling Old Age and able to harrow Hell itself.

Another, more intellectual example: during anima imagining of whatever sort – spiteful, lascivious, or productive – an animus spirit rises up and begins to criticize. Precisely here is the origin of the critical spirit as that part of fantasy which detaches itself, abstracts, makes comparisons, and looks down. This animus serves soul by separating mind from mood to gain distance. However, as an animus bound in tandem with anima, this critical spirit still retains traces of moodiness, now 'objectified' into opinion. So it is not altogether freed of subjectivism. (Little wonder that critics seem anima-ridden and opinionated, both.) The objective spirit, that goal of our Western intellectual endeavor, is an attempt of the soul to free itself by means of the animus from the valley of its attachments. And the figure in dreams who judges is the one who both frees us from anima imprisonments and sentences us with his opinions.

To consider every position in terms of the syzygy reflects a "hermaphroditic" consciousness in which the One and the Other are co-present, a priori, at all times, a hermetic duplicity and aphroditic coupling going on in every event. This works in the following way:

When we feel we have caught a glimpse of anima in an image, mood, or projection, the immediate next question is 'where is animus?' Most likely it is in the perceiving ego itself that has made the observation possible in the first place (i.e., we see the one through the other). Thus *the observation is also a projection*, part of the mutual fantasy system of the anima–animus which the ego does not recognize.

By looking to the ego for the missing other, we can see the ego's attitudes and behaviors as part of a tandem. For example: am I now sun-lit Apollo in my ego (animus) consciousness because Sister Soul is Artemisian, a good clean companion that keeps her distance; or is anima Hyacinthic, a beautiful, dying boy, or Daphnic, a flighty, vegetating symptom, or Dionysian in wet rout. Or, to turn it around the other way: does the anima show Aphrodisian qualities because my ego (animus) attitudes are like Hephaistos hammering away in the heat, or young and chosen Paris, or old Kronos with cut-off sexuality. . . . Endless tandems.

The principal tandem concerns the very qualities by which analytical psychology has been characterizing anima and animus. As long as anima refers to interiority, to reflexive and fantasy functions, to the attached and the personal, then animus must appear in exteriorities, activities, and in literal, impersonal, and objective ways. This sort of pairing inheres in the Latin words themselves where *anima* was the substantive "breath" and *animus* the "activity of breathing." And, as animus is defined in *A Latin Dictionary* (Lewis and Short) with the phrase "the rational soul in man," then anima of course is left to pick up the irrational, emotional, and fantastic. Yet more revealing is that the qualities of *animus* in Latin – activities and functions of consciousness, attention, intellect, mind, will, courage, arrogance, and pride – are those which we nowadays in somewhat different terms attribute to the ego. Indeed, it seems that much of what psychology has been calling ego is the animus-half of the syzygy.

This leads into a job for another time: an examination of the notion of "ego" and a comparison of it with "animus." I suspect that the archetype behind the ego of Western culture as it has issued into ego psychology would reveal itself as the animus, that, in fact, ego is an animus idea. An animus that loses its soul (anima) connection, that posits itself as independent of the syzygy, is ego. The 'weak ego' would be the one affected by the syzygy with anima, and 'strengthening the ego' would mean strengthening the animus. Ego may be heroic in *content*, but as a psychic *function* it derives from animus, enacting particular projections of anima. As a function of the syzygy, ego cannot have a valid identity of its own. If this conjecture were borne out, then we might be able to rearrange much of our psychic furniture. We might structure the psyche without ego, letting this concept drop out and experiencing in its place the imaginal constellations playing through various mythological pairings.

To put all this more succinctly: *syzygy consciousness* is of and within a tandem; it is an awareness of being in a particular pairing, the dynamics of which are best described by myths. (Psychodynamics is one of the things mythology is all about.) *Anima or animus consciousness* would mean recognizing the kind of unconsciousness in any particular constellation, its other archetypal side.

(a) ... we lack all knowledge of the unconscious psyche and pursue the cult of consciousness to the exclusion of all else. Our true religion is a monotheism of consciousness, a possession by it, coupled with a fanatical denial of the existence of fragmentary autonomous systems. CW 13, §51

Ego consciousness would refer to what Jung calls the "monotheism of consciousness,"[a] the single-minded viewpoint of the individual "I," where the other is lost sight of and which results in literalism. Thus, ego consciousness is an unconsciousness of psychic actuality.

Psychic actuality is such that "the two figures are always tempting the ego to identify itself with them" (CW 16, §469). The identification of the conscious ego personality with one of them seems to be the archetypal role the ego is bound to play, since "neither anima nor animus can be constellated without the intervention of the conscious personality" (ibid.). Because they always appear together, it logically follows that the "intervention of the conscious personality" is actually an enacting of anima or animus, the other half.

This is most difficult to recognize because in the conscious personality of the ego is where Jung locates our darkest spot. Sol, the alchemical image of ego consciousness, is itself a "dark body," "light without and darkness within," a *"relatively constant personification of the unconscious itself"* in "the source of [whose] light there is darkness enough for any amount of projections" (CW 14, §129).

Although the conscious personality is relatively constant, it is nevertheless subject to the sudden egressions of intrapsychic projections. However, because of its constancy, these projections, which the ego calls its attitudes, decisions, and positions, are extra-durable, their very constancy making them extra hard to see through. But it is in that opaque spot that we must look for the actual unconscious. The prima materia is ego.

———

Another consequent of the syzygy concerns the soul–spirit relation. Being-in-soul (*esse in anima*) implies being infused with animus, its pneuma, its spirit. The airy aspect of anima discussed above can also be considered anima in syzygy with animus. Being-in-soul, psychological being, implicates spiritual being; spirit will be constellated whenever we are in touch with soul.

This happens often enough in experience. At the very moment of a new psychological move, we hear animus voices driving us

from it by spiritualizing the experience into abstractions, extracting its meaning, carrying it into actions, dogmatizing it into general principles, or using it to prove something. Where anima is vivid, animus enters. Similarly, when at work intellectually, or in spiritual meditation, or where courage is screwed to the sticking place, then anima invades with images and fears, with distractions of attachments and connections, telephoning, natural urges, suicidal despairs, or disturbing with ever deeper questions and puzzling unknowns. Moved by a new idea or spiritual impetus, anima is right there, wanting to make it personal, asking, "How does it relate?" and "What about me?" These torturing incursions of soul into spirit and spirit into soul are the syzygy in action. This is the *coniunctio.*

Because of the anima–animus syzygy, psychology cannot omit spirit from its purview. The syzygy says that where soul goes there goes spirit too. Their syzygy illumines imagination with intellect and refreshens intellect with fantasy. Ideas become psychological experiences, and experiences become psychological ideas. The job is to keep spirit and soul distinct (the spirit's demand) and to keep them attached (the demand of the soul).

Notes

ABBREVIATIONS

CW C. G. Jung, *The Collected Works*, trans. R. F. C. Hull, ed. H. Read, M. Fordham, G. Adler, Wm. McGuire, Bollingen Series XX, vols. 1–20 (Princeton: Princeton University Press and London: Routledge and Kegan Paul, 1953 ff.), paragraph numbers.

MA J. Hillman, *The Myth of Analysis* (Evanston: Northwestern University Press, 1972; New York: Harper & Row, 1978).

RP J. Hillman, *Re-Visioning Psychology* (New York: Harper & Row, 1975).

DU J. Hillman, *The Dream and the Underworld* (New York: Harper & Row, 1979).

1. *A Short List of the Main Literature on Anima*
   A. *From Jung's* CW
      1) Anima-titled writings
      [Psyche, personality, persona, anima]: CW 6, §§797–811; Anima and Animus: CW 7, §§296–340; Concerning the Archetypes, with Special Reference to the Anima Concept: CW 9, i, §§111–47; The Syzygy: Anima and Animus: CW 9, ii, §§20–42; Animus and Anima: CW 13, §§57–63.
      2) From Jung's writings about Anima, but not so titled
      "The Psychological Aspects of the Kore," especially: CW 9, ii, §§306–11, 355–58; *Mysterium Coniunctionis:* CW 14, passim.
      3) Other Jung references from the General Index, CW 20. Clusters of passages on Anima and frequently indexed paragraphs.
      CW 5, §§605–08, 678; CW 7, §§370, 374, 521; CW 9, i, §§53–66, 512–18; CW 9, ii, §§53–59, 422–25; CW 10, §§75–79, 713–15; CW 11, §§47–49, 71–73; CW 12, §§92–94, 112, 116, 192, 394–98; CW 13, §§216–18, 223, 261–63, 453–60; CW 15, §§210–13; CW 16, §§432–38, 454, 469, 504; CW 17, §§338–41.

B. *Anima by classical authors of the Jungian tradition*

H. G. Baynes, *The Mythology of the Soul* (London: Baillière, Tindall & Cox, 1940); E. Bertine, "The Story of Anima Projection" in *Human Relationships* (New York: Longmans, Green, 1958); C. Brunner, *Die Anima als Schicksalsproblem des Mannes* (Zürich: Rascher Verlag, 1963); L. Fierz-David, *The Dream of Poliphilo* (New York: Pantheon, 1950); E. Harding, *The Way of All Women* (New York: Longmans, Green, 1933), pp. 1–40; E. Jung, *Animus and Anima*, trans. C. F. Baynes and H. Nagel (Spring Publications, 1957); E. Jung and M.-L. von Franz, *The Grail Legend* (New York: Putnam's, 1971); J. Layard, "The Incest Taboo and the Virgin Archetype" in *Images of the Untouched* (Dallas: Spring Publications, Inc., 1982); J. Singer, *Boundaries of the Soul* (New York: Doubleday, 1972), chap. 9; M. Stein, ed., *Jungian Analysis* (LaSalle, Il.: 1982), pp. 74–84, 282–91; A. B. Ulanov, *The Feminine in Jungian Psychology and Christian Theology* (Evanston: Northwestern University Press, 1971); M.-L. von Franz, *The Problem of the Feminine in Fairy Tales* (Spring Publications, 1972); M.-L. von Franz, "The Anima" in *Man and His Symbols* (London: Aldus, 1964); E. C. Whitmont, "The Anima" in *The Symbolic Quest* (New York: Putnam's, 1969); F. G. Wickes, *The Inner World of Choice* (New York: Harper & Row, 1963), chap. 11, "The Woman in Man."

C. *Other writings on anima phenomenology by James Hillman*

"Inner Femininity: Anima Reality and Religion" in *Insearch: Psychology and Religion* (New York: Charles Scribner's Sons, 1967; Dallas: Spring Publications, 1979); "Anima and Psyche" in MA; "Pan's Nymphs" in *Pan and the Nightmare* (with W. H. Roscher) (Spring Publications, 1972); "Betrayal" and "Schism" in *Loose Ends: Primary Papers in Archetypal Psychology* (Spring Publications, 1975); RP: q.v. index; J. Hillman, ed., *Puer Papers* (Dallas: Spring Publications, 1979), pp. 38–42, 66–71, 119–21; "Silver and the White Earth," *Spring 1980* and *Spring 1981*; "Alchemical Blue and the *Unio Mentalis*," *Sulfur* 1 (1981); "Salt: A Chapter in Alchemical Psychology" in *Images of the Untouched*; "*Anima Mundi:* The Return of the Soul to the World," *Spring 1982*; *The Thought of the Heart* (Dallas: Spring Publications, 1984), pp. 33–50.

2. *C. G. Jung Letters*, trans. R. F. C. Hull and ed. G. Adler and A. Jaffé, Bollingen Series XCV (Princeton: Princeton University Press, 1973–75), Volume I: Letters 1906–50, Volume II: Letters 1951–1961.

3. For a succinct study of kinds of oppositional pairs and some of the confusions arising when the kinds are not kept distinct, see C. K. Ogden, *Opposition* (1932) (Bloomington: Indiana University Press, 1967).

4. MA, "Toward an Imaginal Ego," pp. 183–90; DU, pp. 55–59.

5. Cf. R. B. Onians, *The Origins of European Thought about the Body, the Mind, the Soul, the World, Time and Fate*, 2d ed. (Cambridge: Cambridge University Press, 1954), chapters "The *Psyche*" and "*Anima* and *Animus*"; F. E. Peters, *Greek Philosophical Terms* (New York: New York University Press,

1967), section "*psyche*"; also my discussions in DU, chapter "Psyche," and in RP, section "Anima" and pp. 44–51.

6. Because of the soul's motility – a prime trait that sometimes even defined soul – some Greek philosophy did associate psyche with fire (Atomists), and Aristotle considered *orexis* (appetite, desire) the ultimate cause of the soul's motion.

7. J. J. Bachofen, *Myth, Religion, and Mother Right: Selected Writings*, Bollingen Series (Princeton: Princeton University Press, 1967), pp. 93 ff. W. H. Roscher, *Lexikon d. Griech. u. Röm. Mythologie* (Hildesheim: Olms, 1965), vol. III, i: "Pan," pp. 1392 f. and "Nymphen," pp. 500 ff. E. Jung, "The Anima as an Elemental Being," in her *Animus and Anima*. Cf. T. Wolff's amplification of the hetaera in connection with the anima: "Strukturformen der weiblichen Psyche," in her *Studien zu C. G. Jung's Psychologie* (Zürich: Daimon Verlag, 1981), pp. 175–76.

8. MA, pp. 61–79; "Peaks and Vales" in *Puer Papers*.

9. C. G. Jung, *Memories, Dreams, Reflections*, recorded and ed. A. Jaffé, trans. R. and C. Winston (New York: Vintage, 1965), p. 286, for Jung's experience and formulation of the historical anima personified in the Galla Placidia incident in Ravenna: "The anima of a man has a strongly historical character."

10. G. Bachelard, *The Poetics of Reverie* (Boston: Beacon Press, 1971), chapter 2, "Animus and Anima."

11. For a brief statement by Corbin on soul and imagination, see H. Corbin, "*Mundus Imaginalis*," *Spring* 1972, pp. 6–7.

12. M. Ficino, *Theologia platonica, XII*, in C. Trinkaus, *In Our Image and Likeness* (Chicago: The University of Chicago Press, 1970), 2:476–78 and notes.

13. Onians, *Origins*, pp. 168–73 with notes.

14. Porphyry, "Concerning the Cave of Nymphs," in *Thomas Taylor the Platonist: Selected Writings*, ed. G. H. Mills and K. Raine, Bollingen Series (Princeton: Princeton University Press, 1969), p. 304. The discourse, too long to quote, is upon nymphs and naiads and the Neoplatonic meaning of the moist element.

15. Further on the aerial anima, see my "The Imagination of Air and the Collapse of Alchemy" in *Eranos Jahrbuch* 50–1981 (Frankfurt a/M: Insel Verlag, 1982), pp. 273–333, and DU, pp. 185–88 on "Smell and Smoke."

16. Bachelard, *Poetics*, p. 66: "*anima* becomes deeper and reigns in descending toward the cave of being. By descending, ever descending, the ontology of the qualities of the *anima* is discovered."

17. Onians, *Origins*, p. 170n.

18. For a fuller discussion, see my "The Feeling Function," Part Two of *Lectures on Jung's Typology* (with M.-L. von Franz) (Spring Publications, 1971), especially, "Feeling and the Anima," pp. 121–29.

19. H. F. Ellenberger, *The Discovery of the Unconscious* (New York: Basic Books, 1970), pp. 199–201.

20. Ibid., p. 233.

21. Ph. Wolff-Windegg, "C. G. Jung – Bachofen, Burckhardt, and Basel,"

Spring 1976, pp. 137–47.

22.   S. Freud, *New Introductory Lectures on Psycho-Analysis* (London: Hogarth, 1957), chapter 33, p. 145.

23.   R. Grinnell, "Reflections on the Archetype of Consciousness: Personality and Psychological Faith," *Spring 1970*, pp. 15–39.

24.   E. Neumann, *The Origins and History of Consciousness*, Bollingen Series (New York: Pantheon, 1954), p. 42.

25.   W. F. Otto, *Die Musen* (Darmstadt, 1954), pp. 9–20.

26.   MA, pp. 49–61; also my *Insearch*, chapter "Inner Femininity."

27.   Two letters bring out the ambiguity of the anima-mother configuration in Jung's own imagery. In a letter to Victor White (30 January 1948), Jung writes that he had his "first anima-experience, the woman that was *not* my mother" when he was three years old. In a letter to Ignaz Tauber (13 December 1960), Jung describes his old-age stone carving of a primitive woman stretching out her hands to the udder of a mare. "The woman is obviously my anima in the guise of a millennia-old ancestress." As there is a need to differentiate anima from mother, so there seems an equal need not to lose their interpenetration.

28.   J. Hillman, "An Essay on Pan," in *Pan and the Nightmare*, pp. xliv–lvi.

29.   I have discussed some of the historical background to the ego notion and its anachronistic retention in analytical psychology in MA, pp. 148–54, 183–90, 279, 290.

30.   J. Layard, "On Psychic Consciousness" (*Eranos Jahrbuch* 1959 [Zürich: Rhein]), reprinted in his *The Virgin Archetype* (Spring Publications, 1972).

31.   All passages here from Onians are found on p. 169 of *Origins*.

32.   Bachelard, *Poetics*, pp. 64, 67.

33.   Cf. D. Henderson and R. D. Gillespie, *A Text Book of Psychiatry* (Oxford: Cumberlege, 1950), p. 128.

34.   J. Drever, *A Dictionary of Psychology* (London: Penguin, 1952), p. 78.

35.   Cf. Onians, *Origins*, pp. 168 ff.; C. T. Lewis and C. Short, *A Latin Dictionary* (Oxford: Clarendon, 1894), "*anima*," pp. 120–21.

36.   Drever, *Dictionary*, p. 62.

37.   Ibid., and also DU, pp. 24–26 et passim, where I have discussed Heraclitus's notion of depth in relation with depth psychology.

38.   RP, pp. 1–51.

39.   H. Corbin, *Avicenna and the Visionary Recital* (Dallas: Spring Publications, 1980), p. 21.

40.   Cf. P. Berry, "On Reduction," in her *Echo's Subtle Body: Contributions to an Archetypal Psychology* (Dallas: Spring Publications, 1982), pp. 163–85, for an examination of the "Philistine literalist" within each of us.

41.   On the disastrous confusions of anima and feeling in notions and in behavior, see chapters two and three above and my "The Feeling Function" in *Lectures on Jung's Typology*, chapter 6.

42.   J. Burnet, *Early Greek Philosophy* (London: Black, 1948), p. 143; according to M. Marcovich, *Heraclitus–Editio Maior* (Merida, Venezuela: Los Andes University Press), only fragments 45 and 47 (Bywater–Burnet) contain the actual word *harmonia*.

43. H. Binswanger, "Positive Aspects of the Animus," *Spring 1963*, pp. 82–101.

44. The complicated development of the Christian idea of soul is traced summarily by H. Robinson in J. Hastings, *Encyclopedia of Religion and Ethics* (Edinburgh: Clark, 1920), 11:733a–737b. A. Hultekrantz, "Seele," *Die Religion in Geschichte und Gegenwart* (Tübingen: Mohr, 1961), 5:1634–636, sees an upward development of the soul idea from the pluralistic souls of primitive peoples, through a dualism of souls, to a "soul-monism" of "high civilisations" (including Christian). The argument echoes the one examined and refused by J. Hillman, "Psychology: Monotheistic or Polytheistic?", *Spring 1971*, pp. 193–208, reprinted with extensions in D. L. Miller, *The New Polytheism* (Dallas: Spring Publications, 1981), pp. 109–42.

45. On schism and heresy as the inevitable consequence of unification, see my "Schism as Differing Visions" in *Loose Ends*, pp. 82–97.

46. The curious intermixture of monocular senex and anima appears in Jung's insight into Kant's categorical imperative (the one single rule on which all morality must be based). In a letter to Gustav Senn on 13 October 1941, Jung writes: "Kant's categorical imperative is of course a philosophical touching-up of a psychic fact which, as you have quite correctly seen, is unquestionably a manifestation of the anima."

47. From a conversation cited in Miguel Serrano, *C. G. Jung and Hermann Hesse: A Record of Two Friendships*, trans. F. MacShane (New York: Schocken, 1968), pp. 50, 56.

48. C. G. Jung, *The Integration of the Personality*, trans. Stanley Dell (London: Kegan Paul, 1940), p. 91.

49. For examples of such syzygies in ordinary life, see my *Insearch*, pp. 96–101.